A KID'S HANDBOOK FOR KEEPING EARTH HEALTHY AND GREEN

I CAN SAVE THE EARTH

ANITA HOLMES

ILLUSTRATED BY
DAVID NEUHAUS

For Alice, Ramón, Edda, Christina, and Jimena

ACKNOWLEDGMENTS

Thanks to my daughter Juliette Soucie for her many good suggestions and help with research. Thanks also to Gary Soucie for reading the manuscript and offering suggestions.

Text copyright © 1993 by Anita Holmes. Illustrations copyright © 1993 by David Neuhaus. Published by arrangement with Pearson Education, Inc.

Designed by Malle N. Whitaker

Houghton Mifflin Edition, 2000

No part of this work may be reproduced or transmitted in any form or by any means, electronic or mechanical, including photocopying or recording, or by any information storage or retrieval system without the prior written permission of the copyright owner unless such copying is expressly permitted by federal copyright law. With the exception of nonprofit transcription into Braille, Houghton Mifflin is not authorized to grant permission for further uses of this work. Permission must be obtained from the individual copyright owner as identified herein. Address requests for permission to make copies of Houghton Mifflin material to School Permissions, 222 Berkeley Street, Boston, MA 02116.

Printed in the U.S.A.

ISBN: 0-395-98833-0

456789–MZ–05 04 03 02 01

Library of Congress Cataloging-in-Publication Data

Holmes, Anita.
   I can save the earth : a kid's handbook for keeping earth healthy and green by Anita Holmes ; illustrated by David Neuhaus.
     p.   cm.
   Includes index.
   Summary: Presents various ways in which everyone can help protect the environment and save the earth.
   1. Environmental protection--Citizen participation—Juvenile literature. 2. Conservation of natural resources—Citizen participation—Juvenile literature. [1. Environmental protection. 2. Conservation of natural resources.] I. Neuhaus, David, III. II. Title.
TD171.7.H65   1993   91-30611
333.7′2—dc20   CIP   AC

ISBN 0-671-74544-1 (LSB)
ISBN 0-671-74545-X (pbk.)

Permission to reprint *The Green Rap* by Caryn Studebaker and *The Eco Rap* by John Thomas Fitzgerald courtesy of *P-3 Magazine* and *Disney Adventures Magazine*.

Help the Air! by Matt Yeates reprinted by permission of *Rethinking Schools*, May/June 1991.

The "Save Water" poster by Brandi Babcock and the "Use Water Wisely" poster by Kim Koehler reprinted through the courtesy of Texas Water Development Board, Austin, TX.

The "Let's Recycle!" poster by Caroline Duncan reprinted by permission of *Cobblestone*, June 1991. The National Road, copyright © 1991, Cobblestone Publishing, Inc., Peterborough, NH.

"Earthbags" courtesy of The Friends of Nature Club, Petaluma, CA.

"City Trees" by Edna St. Vincent Millay. From *Collected Poems*, HarperCollins. Copyright 1921, 1948 by Edna St. Vincent Millay. Reprinted by permission of Elizabeth Barnett, literary executor.

Boston • Atlanta • Dallas • Denver • Geneva, Illinois • Palo Alto • Princeton

KEEPING EARTH CLEAN AND GREEN	4
1 CHOICES, CHOICES, CHOICES	6
2 FOR FRESH AIR	8
3 FOR PURE WATER	22
4 FOR LAND AND RESOURCES	33
5 FOR PLANTS AND PLACES	46
6 FOR ANIMALS	62
7 FOR KID POWER	75
FURTHER READING	87
GLOSSARY	89
INDEX	92

KEEPING EARTH CLEAN AND GREEN

WARNING:

Reading this book could be risky.
It could make you *think* things you've never thought before.
It could make you *do* things you've never done.

Suppose you have a beautiful park of your very own. The park is full of towering trees, colorful flowers, and rolling meadows. Winding paths lead to hidden lakes and streams. Hundreds of wild animals roam freely in your park. You want to share your park with your friends and neighbors. But you worry that too many visitors could ruin it. How could you keep the park beautiful while still allowing everyone to enjoy it?

Perhaps you should make some rules. You might hang up a sign that said:

PLEASE . . .
▲ don't bother the animals.
▲ don't trample the plants.
▲ don't start any fires.
▲ don't litter.
▲ take nothing but photographs.
▲ leave nothing behind but footsteps.

Most people willingly follow park rules like these. They know that carelessness can ruin parks. People know that the only way to enjoy parks is to care enough to keep them clean and green.

But what about the rest of the environment? Shouldn't people treat the entire earth with care too? After all, nature isn't just in parks. Nature is all around us—even in cities.

Wouldn't it be nice to do something special for the earth? This book will show the many things you can do to protect the earth and keep it clean and green.

A WORD ABOUT GREEN

The next time you hike through a forest or visit a park, stop and see which color appears most often. Green, of course.

From the tallest trees to a single blade of grass, green is the color that paints much of the outdoors. Green is the color of nature. This is why friends of the earth often say, "Keep earth green." When you protect nature, you're helping to keep the earth green and healthy.

CHAPTER 1
CHOICES, CHOICES, CHOICES

THE GREEN RAP

Too many people just don't care.
They're polluting our oceans and air.
Birds aren't flyin', fish are dyin'
'cause too many people just aren't tryin'
to make this earth a better place for you and me,
that's right, planet 3.
The ecosystem's fallin' apart,
people need to have a change of heart.
We've come from the start
but aren't quite done
till this earth is #1!!

Caryn Studebaker
Dutton, VA

DID YOU KNOW?

Our ENVIRONMENT is everything that surrounds us. It's land and water and air, and everything that's on the land and in the water and air. People are part of the environment. So are plants and animals.

Take a walk through a busy city. Visit a factory area. Ride along a superhighway that passes a factory or garbage dump. It's easy to see that many parts of the earth aren't green and healthy. In many places people have cut down forests. In lots of places people have polluted air and soil and water. In other places people have thrown trash all around. Many parts of the earth are in big trouble. Many parts aren't even fit to live in.

WHAT CAN YOU DO?

Here are some choices. You can . . .

a. cry and do nothing. After all, you're just a kid.

b. wish upon a star that things will change.

c. become a friend of the earth and find out what you can do to help.

WHAT WILL HAPPEN?

Suppose you choose answer **a.** If you only cry and do nothing, things will never change. The earth will keep having problems.

Suppose you choose answer **b.** What are the chances that your wish will be answered by a star: one in a thousand? one in a million? no chance at all? You're in for a long wait if you count on getting that wish.

Now suppose you choose answer **c.** You're just one person. Can one earth-loving person make a difference? Yes! And if that earth-loving person has a few friends who think the same, then watch out. Exciting things can happen!

CHOOSING TO BE AN EARTH FRIEND

To say you're a friend of the earth is easy. Being such a friend is not always easy. It sometimes takes work. Sometimes it costs money. Often it takes time. Here's an example.

You're walking along the street. You unwrap a candy bar. What will you do with the candy wrapper?

You could put it in your pocket. But you probably don't want candy wrappers in your pockets.

You could throw it in a trash can. But that's work and may take time. You'll have to hunt for a trash can. Maybe you'll have to walk across the street to get to it.

It would be easier just to throw the wrapper on the street. But this isn't very earth-friendly.

Each day we make choices. Many of our choices can hurt the earth. Other choices can help save it. What to do with litter is just one of those choices.

This book can help you make choices that help the earth. But first you must decide that saving the earth is important to you.

ONE IS A LOT

You're just one person. Can you make a difference? Do your actions count? You bet.

Why? First, because your actions can help change the actions of others. And this can lead to good things for the earth. Second, because many is a whole lot of ones. And a lot of ones, that is, single individuals, add up. Soon a powerful group of friends of the earth develops.

When someone throws litter on the ground and someone else comes along and copies that litterbug, that soon adds up to a lot of litter. But in the same way, if you pick up some litter and your friend sees you and decides to help, the earth begins to look cleaner and greener.

What you do on earth **is** important. What you do **can** help!

CHAPTER 2
FOR FRESH AIR

AIR

Blue sky
Turns into smoggy sky.
You can't see the horizon.
Trees are putting up with the misery.
The cycle is not working.
People are not caring.
They think it is not their responsibility.
They just bring in the exhaust.
What do they care?
HELP THE AIR!

Matt Yeates
Sacramento, California

You can't see it.
You can't hold it.
When it's clean, you can't smell or taste it.
But it is all around you.
What is it?
Of course, it's air.

Air might be invisible, but it's plenty important. It creates wind, and it moves heat and rain around the world. *And* it contains oxygen—the gas we need to breathe.

NOT SO FRESH!

Take a deep breath. Let the air fill your lungs. Clean, fresh air is great—full of life-giving oxygen. But what if the air is not so fresh—what if it's polluted?

Air pollution can make people sick. It makes things dirty. It can damage buildings, forests, and streams. It can kill plants.

Air pollution can even change the weather. It can trap heat and make the air warmer than it should be. It can "chew" holes in the atmosphere. It can mix with clouds to form poisonous acid rain.

WHAT POLLUTES THE AIR?

▲ Everything that burns pollutes. We burn wood, coal, and other fuels for heat. We burn gasoline to make cars go. We burn trash to get rid of it. We burn charcoal to cook with. All of this burning puts smoke into the air—and smoke spells pollution.
▲ Fumes from paints, cleaners, glues, and other chemical products also pollute.
▲ Certain dusts and particles pollute too.

First, you can do what Matt Yeates writes about in his poem. You can *care*. If you care, you'll learn what causes pollution. Then you'll try to prevent it. The next pages contain some good ideas on how to help the air.

DID YOU KNOW?

Air is a mixture of many gases. OXYGEN and CARBON DIOXIDE are two of the gases in air. The oxygen in air is what we breathe. We take about twenty thousand breaths a day. Carbon dioxide is a gas that we breathe out. It is a waste gas.

A WORD ABOUT ENERGY

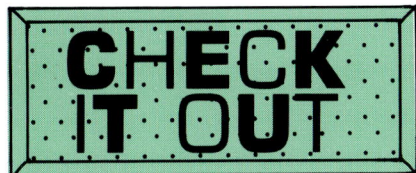

Do you have lots of energy? Energy is the strength or power to move or do something. You need energy to do anything: to run, to jump, to walk, to read, to write, even to sleep and breathe. People get their energy from food.

People invented machines to help them do their work. Machines need energy too. Machines get their energy from fuel: gasoline, kerosene, oil, and coal. And this creates a problem for earth. Why? When machines burn fuels, they cause pollution.

CHECK IT OUT

Is the air around you clean or dirty? Make a pollution catcher to find out. Here's how.

1. Get some index cards and smear them with petroleum jelly.
2. Thumbtack the cards somewhere outside.
3. After a day or two, look at the cards closely. Are the cards still white? What do you think caused the change?

How's the air in your house? Make an indoor pollution checker to find out. Here's how.

1. Get some white facial tissues. Place a piece over the end of a vacuum-cleaner hose. Use a rubber band to hold it in place.
2. Turn on the vacuum cleaner. Wave the hose through the air for a minute or two.
3. Remove the tissue. Is it still clean? What could be the explanation?

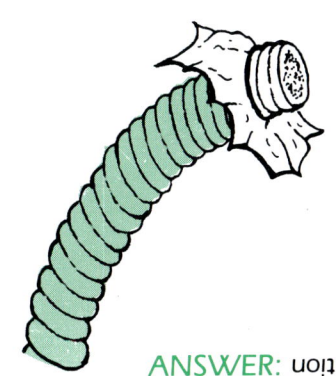

ANSWER: Air Pollution

I CAN... GIVE THE CAR A REST

"Dad, will you give me a lift to school?"

"Mom, please take me to the store."

How many times a week do you ask an adult to drive you somewhere? How many of these trips are short enough so that you could walk or ride your bike? Most people use their cars too much—even for short trips. That's a problem. Why? When a car burns gas, it produces exhaust. And that exhaust pollutes the atmosphere.

WHAT CAN YOU DO?

You can stop asking for so many rides.

FOR SHORT TRIPS...
▲ ride a bike. It's fun. It will help you stay in shape.
▲ skate. You'll wow your friends.
▲ walk (or run). Your two strong legs can take you anywhere.

FOR LONGER TRIPS...
▲ think "combo." Need to go to the store? Want to visit a friend? Have to get your hair cut? Combine them all into one trip.
▲ carpool. You need a ride to sports practice. John and Karen need rides there too. If you get one adult to take all of you, you'll save gas.
▲ take the bus, train, or subway. They can carry a lot of people. And they use much less fuel than if everyone took a separate car.

DID YOU KNOW?

Carbon dioxide is a natural part of air. It is not harmful to breathe. But too much carbon dioxide causes the air around the earth to trap heat from the sun. This causes a climate problem called GLOBAL WARMING.

DID YOU KNOW?

Gasoline is made from oil. More than half the world's oil is used to fuel cars, trucks, and other vehicles.

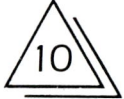

TEST IT OUT

It doesn't take much energy at all to make a bike go. But it (and you) have to be in good shape. To get your bike in shape, clean and oil the moving parts often. This will make them easy to move. Also, keep the tires filled with air. You'll have less trouble pumping the pedals.

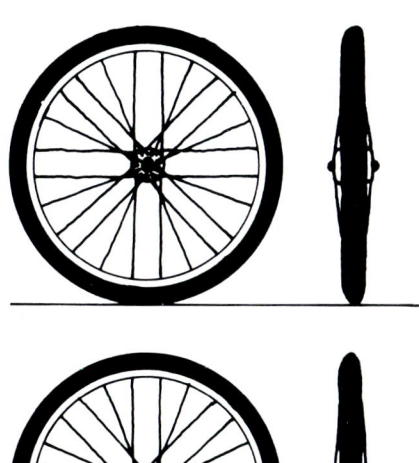

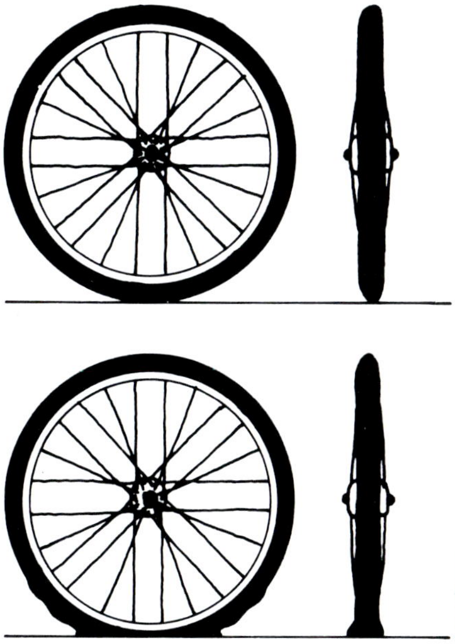

I CAN... BE AN ELECTRICITY "SCROOGE"

You flick a switch. Electricity flows into your lamp and lights the room. But where did the electricity come from?

Electricity has to be made at an electric power plant. Some power plants use flowing water to make electricity. But most use fuel—usually coal or oil. So when you use electricity, you're usually burning fuel. And again you're polluting the air. This is why you should not waste electricity, right?

DID YOU KNOW?

ENERGY is the power to move or do something. Think of all the movement around you: people running, walking, jumping; wheels spinning; plants growing. Energy is needed to make each activity happen. People get energy from food. Plants get energy from sunshine. Cars and machines get energy from fuel.

DID YOU KNOW?

People in the United States use energy in many ways. The following graph shows the main ways we use oil.

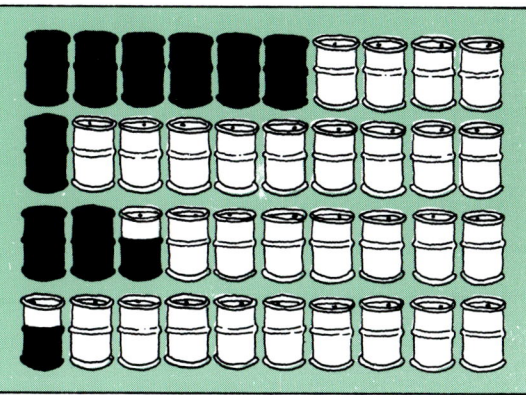

FOR TRANSPORTATION (about 6 out of every 10 barrels)

FOR HOMES (about 1 out of every 10 barrels)

FOR INDUSTRIES AND FARMS (about $2\frac{1}{2}$ out of every 10 barrels)

TO MAKE ELECTRICITY (about $\frac{1}{2}$ out of every 10 barrels)

WHAT CAN YOU DO?

▲ Turn off lights when you leave a room, even if you'll only be gone for a short time. Be sure to turn off the TV, stereo, or radio, too.
▲ Don't use electric power when you can use muscle power.
▲ Always use the right appliance for the job. Want some toast? Use the toaster, not the broiler. Smaller appliances use less energy.
▲ Open and close the refrigerator door as little and as quickly as possible.
▲ Remind your parents to run clothes washers and dishwashers only when they are fully loaded.
▲ Run your clothes dryer just long enough to dry the clothes. Or better yet, hang clothes on a line to dry.
▲ Use the hair dryer only for special occasions. Other times let nature do the job.

DID YOU KNOW?

In some places, coal is burned to make electricity. The burning coal releases harmful gases into the air. When these gases mix with rain, the rain becomes poisonous. We call this ACID RAIN.

Every time you open the refrigerator door, cold air escapes and warm air goes in. Then the refrigerator has to use more electricity to recool the air. Keep track of the number of times you open and close the refrigerator each day. Then try to beat your record.

DID YOU KNOW?

Electricity is measured in WATTS and KILOWATTS. A kilowatt is 1,000 times more powerful than a watt. A clock uses about 2 watts of electricity per hour.

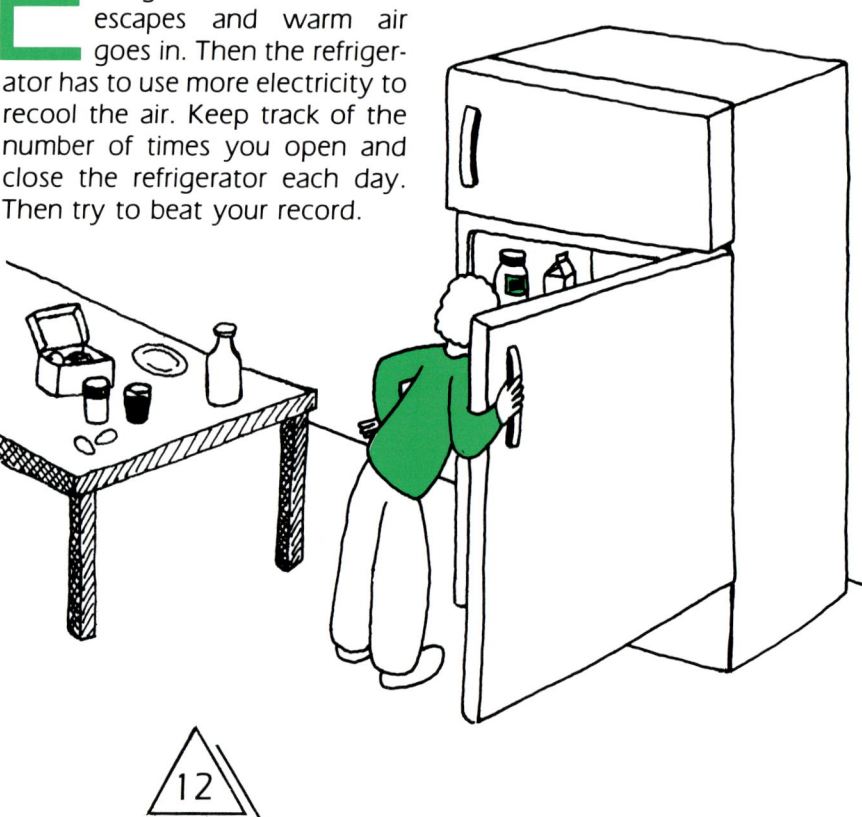

CHECK IT OUT

How much energy does your household use? Try this experiment, *but get an adult's help.*

Shut off all the lights and appliances in the house. Leave on only those that are constantly running—the refrigerator and the clocks. Check the electric meter. Note how fast it's turning. (The meter measures the amount of electricity you're using.)

Next, turn on all the lights in the house. Also turn on the radio, TV, and other appliances. Check the meter again. How fast is it turning now? This should give you an idea of how much electricity your house runs on.

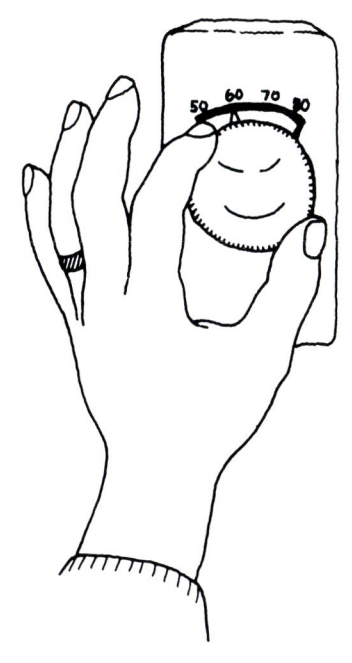

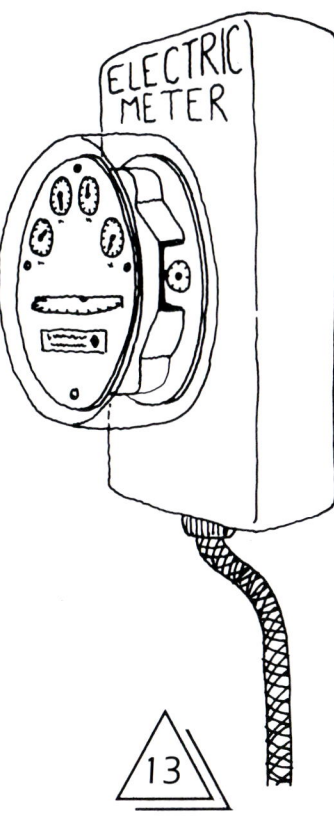

I CAN... WATCH THE TEMPERATURE

How's the temperature in your home? Pretty cozy? Did you know that this coziness doesn't come naturally? Most likely the air in your house is heated or cooled by machines—heaters, furnaces, fans, and air conditioners. It takes lots of energy to keep the temperature comfortable indoors.

DID YOU KNOW?

Several layers of clothes are warmer than one thick layer. The layers of cloth trap heat. Layers of materials in our houses also hold in heat or keep it out. We call such layers INSULATION. The walls, basements, and attics of many homes are stuffed with insulation. It takes less energy to heat such homes.

WHAT CAN YOU DO?

IN WINTER...

▲ go in and out of doors quickly and shut them tightly. Don't let heat escape out the door.

▲ keep windows closed. And try this neat trick with curtains, drapes, and shades. Close them at night and on cloudy days to *keep in* heat. Open them wide on sunny days to *let in* heat.

▲ keep the thermostat turned down. If you feel cold during the day, don't turn up the heat. Put on a sweater.

▲ ask your parents to turn down the thermostat even lower at night—to 55 degrees. If you're cold, add more blankets to the bed.

▲ check for drafts around doors and windows. The cold air escaping wastes energy. Offer to help an adult plug up the leaks. Hardware stores sell products for the job, but in a pinch you can use strips of rags.

IN SUMMER...

▲ close drapes, curtains, and shades during the sunny part of the day. Why? To keep out heat.

▲ if you use an air conditioner, turn it on low. Better yet, use a fan.

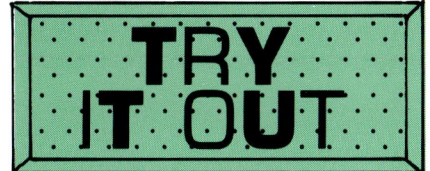

Make a "draft snake" to block out cold drafts.

1. Get some colorful cloth, scissors, needle and thread, dry sand or sawdust, and some felt and buttons for decoration.
2. Cut the cloth into a long rectangle, about 10 inches wide and 40 inches long.
3. Fold the cloth the long way with the right sides of the material together.
4. Sew around the edges of the material. (Use small stitches.) Leave only a four-inch opening at one end.
5. Turn the material right side out and fill it with sand or sawdust.
6. Sew up the opening.
7. Sew on buttons for eyes and pieces of felt for a mouth and tongue.
8. Press the snake snugly beneath a door or window to stop drafts.

DID YOU KNOW?

A $\frac{1}{4}$-inch crack under a door lets out as much heat as a 3-by-3-inch hole.

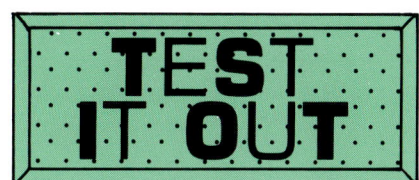

Does heat escape through openings? Try this.

1. Get two glass jars and fill them with hot water.
2. Put a cap on one jar. Leave the other jar uncapped.
3. Wrap both jars with a scarf or towel.
4. After 30 minutes, use a thermometer to test the temperature of the water in each jar. What do you discover?

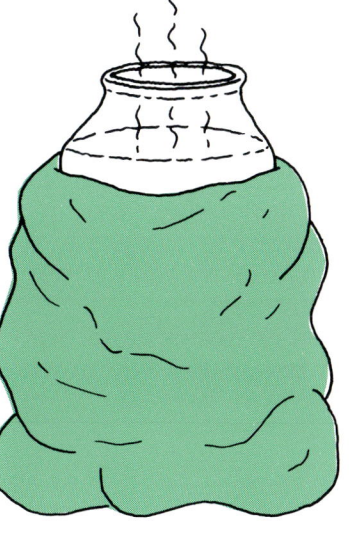
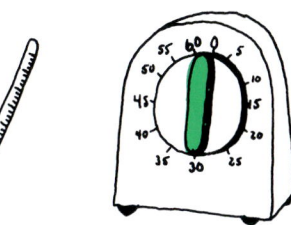

ANSWER: The water in the jar that was capped has remained hot; the water in the jar that was uncapped has cooled off.

I CAN... SAVE HOT WATER

When you turn on the hot water faucet, you probably do not think about how lucky you are. But did you know that long ago houses did not have running hot water? When people wanted a hot bath, they filled buckets of water and heated it over a fire. Then they carried the water to a tub. You can guess that people long ago didn't waste hot water . . . or take many baths!

Now, of course, most American homes have running hot water. It takes a lot of energy to heat water.

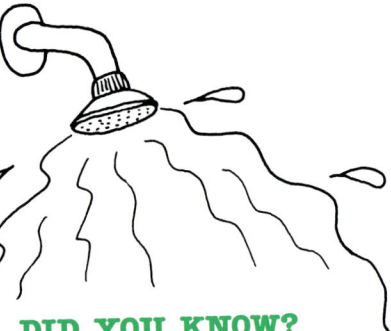

DID YOU KNOW?

Which are the biggest hot water guzzlers? Here's the lowdown.
Deep bath — 36 gallons
Shallow bath — 20 gallons
5-minute shower — 25–35 gallons (5–7 gallons per minute)
Washing hands with hot water running — 2 gallons
Washing dishes with hot water running — 20 gallons
Dishwasher — 10 gallons
Washing machine — 32–59 gallons per cycle

WHAT CAN YOU DO?

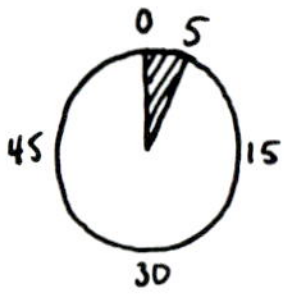

▲ Take shallow baths, not deep ones. To save even more hot water, take a shower—and keep it short.
▲ Don't let the hot water run while you're doing the dishes. It goes right down the drain. Instead, fill a basin to do the job.
▲ Offer to help an adult check for hot water leaks.
▲ Use cold or warm water instead of hot water to wash clothes.

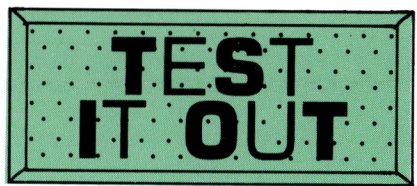
TEST IT OUT

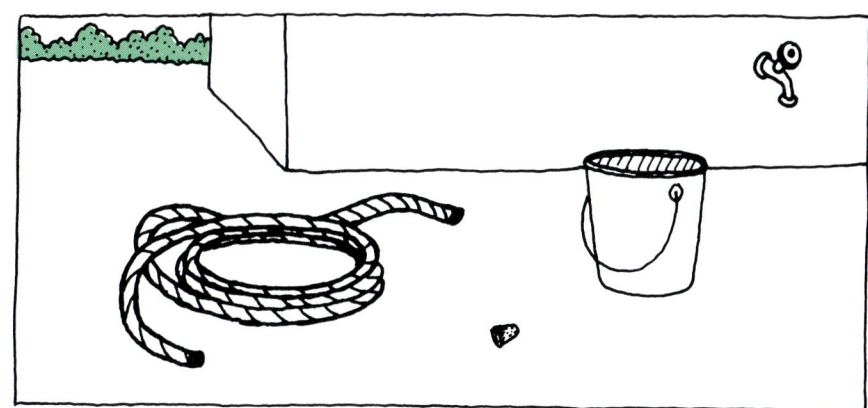

Sunshine is free energy. And it doesn't pollute. Can the sun make water hot enough to use? Try using solar energy to heat your own water, as in the following experiment:

1. Get a garden hose, a cork or other type of plug, and a bucket.
2. On a sunny day, turn on the tap and fill the hose with cold water.
3. Put a plug in the free end of the hose and coil the hose and leave it in the sun.
4. After an hour, remove the plug. How hot is the water? Could you use it to bathe a pet or wash the car?

ANSWER: You bet!

I CAN...
SAY "NO" TO ALL THOSE AIR SPOILERS

WARNING

KEEP OUT OF THE REACH OF CHILDREN.

Avoid breathing of vapors.
Use only in WELL-VENTILATED areas.
When possible, use outdoors.
Do not use in small rooms, closets, or bathrooms.
Use ONLY as directed: Inhaling the contents can be harmful or fatal.

When the container of a product has a warning like this, you can bet that it is not good for the air. Yet many common products such as paint, glue, bug spray, household cleaners, and spot removers carry these warnings. You probably have several of these products in your house. We use them every day. But most are made of chemicals that pollute the air.

WHAT CAN YOU DO?

▲ Make a chemical check of your home. Get an adult's help. Examine the labels on all the products your family uses. If a product contains warning labels like those above, try to find an earth-friendly product to use instead.

▲ Unless absolutely necessary, don't use things that come in aerosol cans. If you need to spray something, use products that come in pump sprayers instead. Regular air makes sprayers work.

▲ Got a bug problem: flies in the house? fleas on the dog? Don't use a chemical bug spray. Use a natural pest spray instead. Or handle the problem in another way. Use soap and water to wash insects off plants and animals. Use a flyswatter for flies—and keep doors and windows shut.

A WORD ABOUT CIGARETTES

Cigarettes are big air spoilers. They contain many poisonous gases that harm our health. They also stink and make things dirty. And they aren't just bad for the smoker. They are bad for everyone around the smoker.

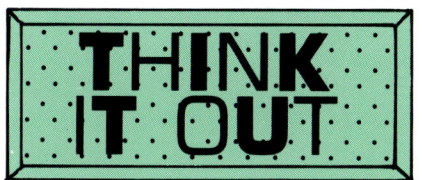

It's never too early to make some decisions about smoking.

▲ If you've ever thought about smoking, promise yourself that you never will.
▲ If those you love smoke, try to get them to stop. But be understanding. Once a person starts smoking, it's hard to give up this bad habit.

DID YOU KNOW?

Tobacco smoke is a main indoor air pollutant. About 467,000 tons of tobacco are burned indoors every year.

I CAN... PROTECT THE AIRWAVES

Sit quietly for a moment. Listen for sounds near and far. What do you hear? Are these sounds pleasant or unpleasant? There's another kind of pollution filling our air: noise. Loud jets roar overhead. Huge trucks thunder by. Car brakes screech. These are some of the annoying outdoor sounds.

There are harsh sounds inside too: music playing too loud, a blaring TV, banging doors, whirring mixers, churning dishwashers. It all hurts the ears . . . and jangles the nerves.

WHAT CAN YOU DO?

▲ Keep the music and the TV sound low.
▲ Close doors softly.
▲ Muffle your voice. Don't shout when talking will do.
▲ Don't run and stomp in the house.
▲ Put a padded rug on the floor in your room. You'll be amazed at how much sound it soaks up.

DID YOU KNOW?

About 10 to 30 miles above the earth there is a wide strip of air called the OZONE LAYER. This layer of air protects us from the dangerous rays of the sun. At least it once did. But now we know that certain chemical gases "chew" holes in the ozone layer.

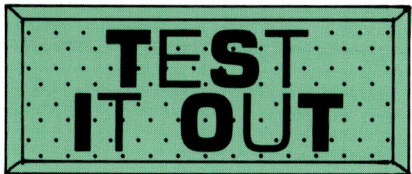

Can a rug muffle sound? Try this.

1. Get a metal bucket.
2. Drop it on an uncovered floor. How would you describe the sound?
3. Drop the bucket on a carpet or padded rug. How does this sound compare?

WHAT'S THE DIFFERENCE?

▲ Here's an "eco-problem" to tease your brain. Suppose you live one mile from the store and you ride in the car to and from the store once a day. In a year's time, you'll make 365 trips to the store and back. That's 730 miles in all!

1 + 1 = 2 miles round trip
2 miles × 365 (days in the year)
= 730 miles

Now think about this. A car goes about 20 miles on a gallon of gas. So to go these 730 miles, you'll need to burn more than 36 gallons of gas.

730 miles ÷ 20 miles a gallon
= $36\frac{1}{2}$ gallons

So what's the big deal? When burned, a gallon of gas produces 20 pounds of carbon dioxide. So $36\frac{1}{2}$ gallons of gas produce 730 pounds of carbon dioxide.

$36\frac{1}{2}$ gallons of gas
× 20 pounds of carbon dioxide
= 730 pounds of carbon dioxide

That's a lot of pollution just to go to the store and back. If you walked or biked instead, how much pollution would you be keeping from poisoning our air?

▲ Suppose everyone in the United States lowered the thermostats in his or her home just three degrees. People would save enough energy to heat more than five million homes. That's as many homes as there are in Illinois, Indiana, and Wisconsin! Even better, this would also reduce air pollution.

CHAPTER 3
FOR PURE WATER

BRANDI BABCOCK
Mauriceville, Texas

KIM KOEHLER,
Comal, Texas

Our planet is a watery place. We call it Earth. But we could just as well call it "Water." More of the earth is covered by water than by land.

You don't believe it? Check out a map of the world. How much of the map shows blue water? You would think that on such a watery planet there would be plenty of fresh water for everybody. But this isn't so. Did you know that about 97 percent of the world's water is in the oceans? And this salty ocean water cannot be used for drinking or growing crops.

Only a small part of earth's water is fresh, or good to drink. You can find fresh water in lakes and ponds, rivers and streams, and underground.

Water is needed by all forms of life. Most of us are lucky—we turn on a faucet and out flows fresh water. But taking our water supply for granted is foolish. In some places water is scarce and people have to ration it. And every day water is getting scarcer. More people are born each year, but the amount of water on the earth stays the same.

What's even more serious is this. People everywhere waste water, or worse, they pollute it. In some places water is no longer fit to drink.

DID YOU KNOW?

People in the United States use more than 90 billion gallons of fresh water a day!

WHAT POLLUTES WATER?

▲ The wastes that get dumped into water pollute.

▲ The wastes that get dumped on land pollute. They seep into groundwater or get carried to bodies of water by rain.

▲ Even dirty air pollutes water. Poisonous gases and soot from power plants, factories, homes and cars are released into the air, where they sometimes mix with clouds. When it rains, these harmful chemicals fall down on the earth and into bodies of water.

WHAT CAN YOU DO?

Brandi Babcock has the right idea. Brandi's poster (see pg. 22) says it. "Save water." That means don't waste it. Just as important, you can keep water clean. That means don't pollute it. In the following pages are some ideas on how to do both.

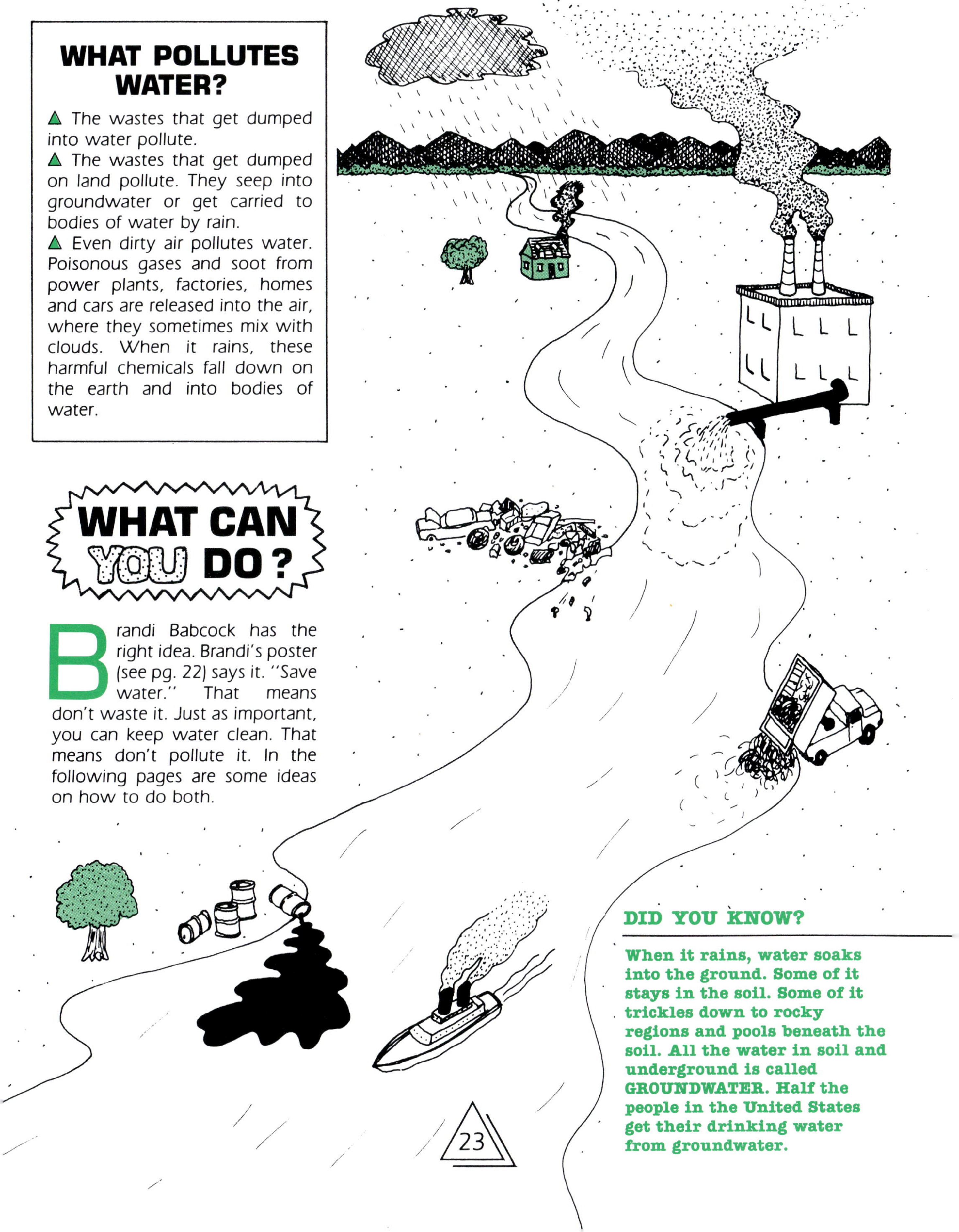

DID YOU KNOW?

When it rains, water soaks into the ground. Some of it stays in the soil. Some of it trickles down to rocky regions and pools beneath the soil. All the water in soil and underground is called **GROUNDWATER**. Half the people in the United States get their drinking water from groundwater.

A WORD ABOUT RAIN

"Oh, no. It's raining. Now they'll cancel the game," you groan to your friend. Do you sometimes complain about the rain? The next time you do, remember this: All the fresh water in our lakes, ponds, streams, and rivers fell to the earth as rain. So did all the water that is contained in the ground. Rain can drown out a ball game, and it can cause more serious problems, such as floods and hurricanes. But if it weren't for rainfall, we'd all be in big trouble.

CHECK IT OUT

Go on a water hunt. Discover how many ways your family uses water at home. Take a walk through your neighborhood to track down more water uses. Bring a small pad and pencil with you. Jot down as many ways as you can think of to save and protect your local water. Does anyone constantly have a sprinkler on—even when it's raining? Does anyone hose used motor oil out of the driveway? What suggestions could you offer?

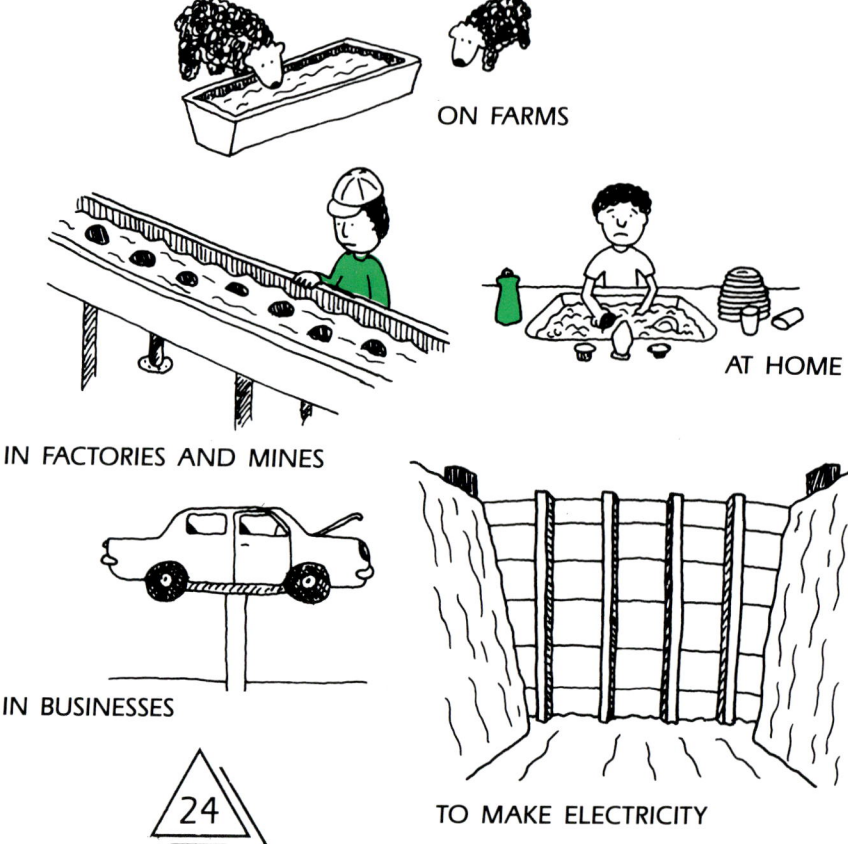

ON FARMS

IN FACTORIES AND MINES

AT HOME

IN BUSINESSES

TO MAKE ELECTRICITY

Where does your water come from: a lake? a reservoir? a river? a well? Ask your parents or a teacher. Or find out at the library. Then use a local map to track the path the water takes to get to your home.

DID YOU KNOW?

People can take salt out of ocean water to make it fresh. In some desert areas, this is done in huge salt-removal plants.

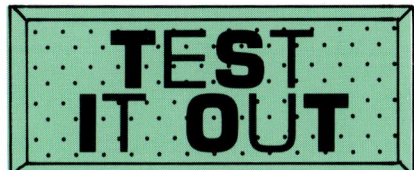

You know that many animals live in fresh bodies of water: Frogs, turtles, snakes, fish, and beavers are only some of them. Many water insects such as dragonflies also live in or near fresh water. Want to find some? Use a dip net to catch some. You can buy a dip net or make one out of a fishnet. Here's how.

1. Get a fishnet, cheesecloth, scissors, string, and an embroidery needle.
2. Cut a triangle of cheesecloth.
3. Make a cheesecloth cone to fit inside the fishnet.
4. Use the string and embroidery needle to sew the cone in place.

Drag your dip net through the water to catch creatures. Empty what you catch into a bucket. Observe the creatures for several minutes; then release them into their watery home. Are these creatures another reason to protect water?

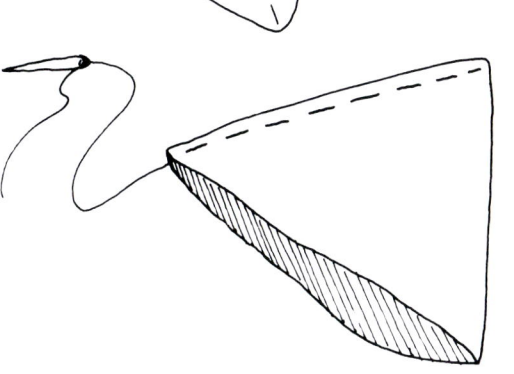

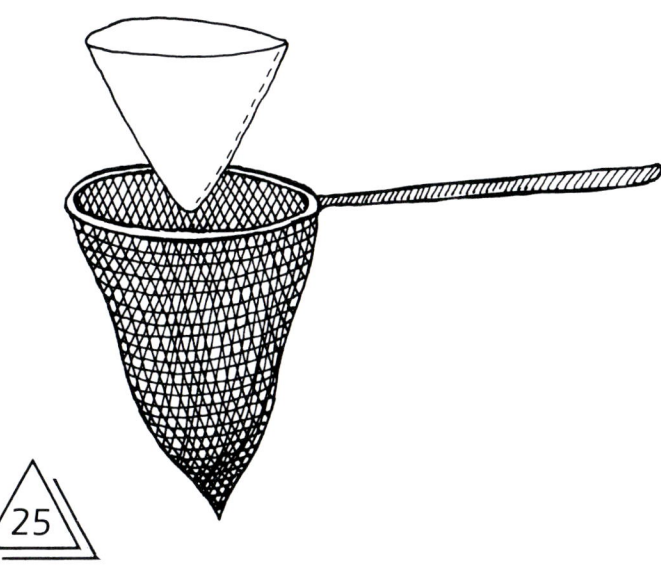

25

I CAN...
BE A WATER "SCROOGE"

Are you a typical American? Then chances are you waste many gallons of water each day. Think about this. Do you leave the water running when you brush your teeth? This is a waste of water. Do you take long showers or deep baths? This wastes water too. The chart shows how much water people use for ordinary morning tasks. And these are only a few of the ways people waste water.

WHAT CAN YOU DO?

▲ Don't leave water running when you aren't using it. Instead of running water while you brush your teeth, do this. Wet your brush. Then turn off the water. Put toothpaste on your brush. Don't turn the water on again until it's time to rinse. Follow this example when you wash your hands or do the dishes.
▲ Don't use the toilet bowl as a wastebasket.
▲ Take quick showers instead of baths.
▲ Do you let the water run down the drain while you're waiting for it to warm up? Instead, catch the water in a bucket or pan and use it for other tasks.

▲ Keep a bottle of water in the refrigerator for drinking. Then you won't have to let the water from the tap run to get cold water.
▲ Is it your turn to water the lawn or garden? Then don't drown your grass or plants. Most lawns and gardens need only 1 to $1\frac{1}{2}$ inches of water a week. If it rains during the week, they may need no water at all.
▲ Like to earn extra money by washing the car? Use a bucket of soapy water instead of letting the hose run. Hose off the car only when you've finished lathering it with soap.

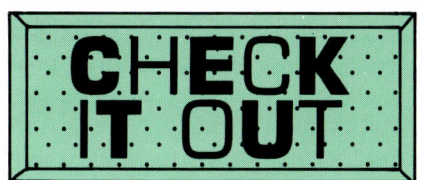
CHECK IT OUT

Do you use more water to shower or bathe? It's easy to figure out, if you have a shower in your tub. Here's how.

1. On day 1, take a bath. Use crayon or tape to mark the height of the water in the tub.

2. On day 2, plug the bathtub drain. Then take a normal shower. Compare the height of the shower water to the height of the bath water you poured the day before.

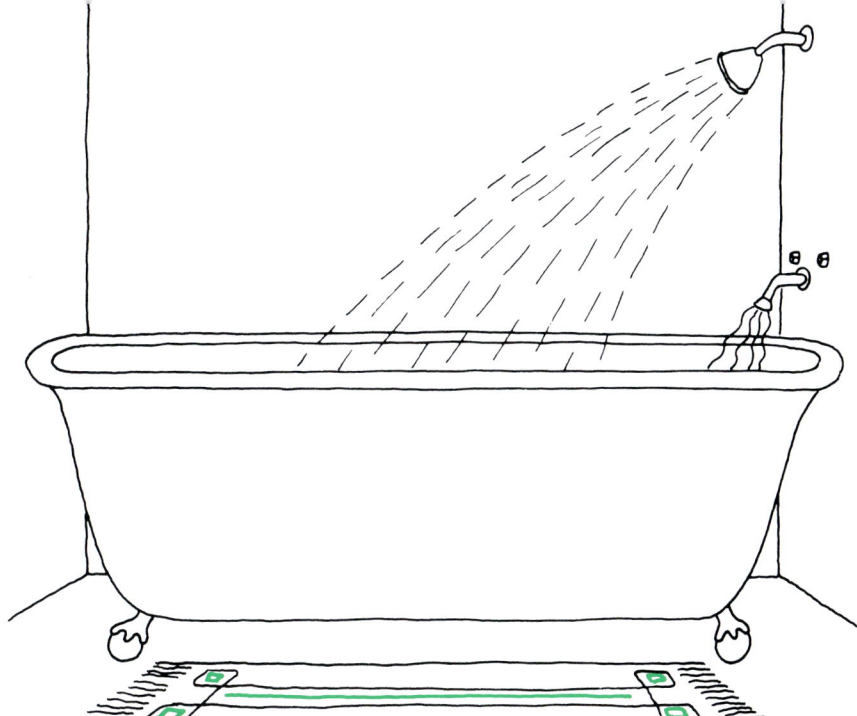

I CAN...
TRACK DOWN LEAKS

Drip, drip, drip. The faucet is leaking, but only a bit. No need to worry, right? Wrong—that dripping faucet and leaky toilet waste a lot of water.

WHAT CAN YOU DO?

▲ Check all the faucets in the house. If you find one that drips, tell your parents.

▲ Check your toilet. If you hear water running in the tank when no one's using it, it's leaking. Again, tell the folks.

DID YOU KNOW?

About 7 out of 10 gallons of water used at home are used in the bathroom. And 4 out of these 7 gallons are flushed down the toilet. If you flush the toilet 5 times, you will use enough water to fill the bathtub.

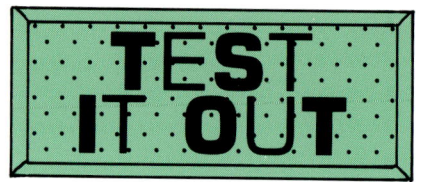
TEST IT OUT

Want to prove if the toilet is leaking or not? Do this experiment, but get an adult to help you.

1. Get some food coloring.
2. Remove the toilet tank top.
3. Put a few drops of food coloring in the tank.
4. Wait 15 minutes. Make sure no one flushes in the meantime. Check the toilet bowl. If colored water shows up, you know you have a leak.

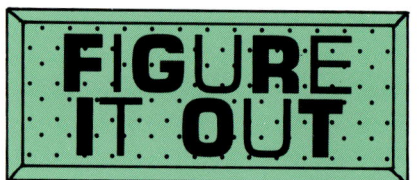
FIGURE IT OUT

Use a measuring cup to check how much water leaks from a faucet in one minute. Then figure out how much water you would lose if the faucet dripped for one hour (60 minutes). For one day (1,440 minutes). For one year (525,600 minutes).

And don't forget to use the water you've collected to water a plant.

I CAN... SAY "NO" TO HARMFUL CLEANERS

Years ago, about the only cleaners people used were soaps. They used soap flakes or a bar of soap to wash everything.

Today, we have special cleaners for each task. We use deodorant soaps to clean our bodies. We use shampoos for our hair. We use washing detergents, bleaches, and fabric softeners for our clothes. We use dishwashing detergents for our dishes and other cleaners for walls, floors, and bathrooms.

So what's wrong with being squeaky clean? Nothing. But some of the cleaners you use might harm the earth. Many modern cleaners work well—but most are made with harmful chemicals. Some of these chemicals flow down the drain and pollute the water. Some also pollute the air. Old-fashioned soap, on the other hand, is pretty harmless.

WHAT CAN YOU DO?

▲ When it comes to detergents and other cleaners, a little goes a long way. Use only as much cleaner as you need to get the job done.

▲ Use old-fashioned soap instead of detergents whenever possible.

▲ If you must use detergents, use ones that say "no phosphates." Phosphates are chemicals that cause green scum (algae) to form on lakes and streams. Too much algae makes water unfit for most creatures to live in.

▲ Forget all those fancy, all-purpose cleaners. For tough jobs use hot water, soap, baking soda or table salt, a brush, and a little muscle power.

▲ Forget all those expensive toilet cleaners too. Use a mixture of vinegar and water instead.

▲ Buy earth-friendly products. These don't hurt the earth. For more information about soap and detergent products that are friendly to the environment, write to:

The Ecology Center
2530 San Paulo Avenue
Berkeley, CA 94702

DID YOU KNOW?

Old-fashion soap doesn't work very well in hard water (water that is loaded with minerals). But you can soften hard water with washing soda or baking soda. Both of these products are EARTH-FRIENDLY.

DID YOU KNOW?

Old-fashioned soap is made of fat and lye. Lye is a chemical found in ashes. Detergents are made from petroleum (oil) products.

TEST IT OUT

Here's an old-fashioned way to wash your dirty socks by hand.

1. Get washing or baking soda and a bar of soap, or soap flakes.
2. Put a small amount of washing or baking soda in a basin of hot water.
3. Add the soap and swish around to make suds.
4. Add your socks and scrub them well.
5. Rinse the socks in fresh water and hang them on a line to dry.

29

DID YOU KNOW?

Water is always moving—downward. Most will someday end up in the ocean. How? When rain falls, some water soaks into the ground. Some runs downhill and flows into streams. These flow into rivers. Rivers carry water to the ocean.

I CAN... WATCH WHAT I DUMP AND WHERE I DUMP IT

Imagine that you have just poured yourself a nice cool glass of water. Suddenly, someone puts a drop of motor oil in it. Another person gives it a shot of paint thinner. Another adds a dash of battery acid. Are you still thirsty for that glass of water?

Yuck! Of course not. No one would be silly enough to dump such things in a glass of water, right? So why do people dump these things down the drain or outside where rain can carry them into our water supply?

Here are some of the poisonous things that get into our water supply:

    cleaning fluids
    dyes
    fingernail polish remover
    gasoline
    glues
    medicines
    motor oil
    paints
    paint thinners
    pesticides
    polishes and varnishes
    spot removers

WHAT CAN YOU DO?

▲ Never use the toilet or kitchen or bathroom sink as a dump for chemicals.
▲ Don't throw chemicals into the yard or the street.
▲ Find out where harmful chemicals should be disposed of in your community. Have your parents take them there.
▲ Until you're ready to get rid of a chemical, put a lid on it. Then store it in a safe spot in your garage or basement.

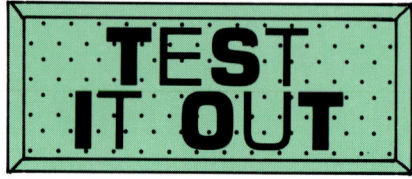

TEST IT OUT

Can polluted water hurt plants? Try this.

1. Dig up two clumps of grass.
2. Put each in its own pot. Then set the pots side by side in a sunny place.
3. Water one plant with fresh water. Water the other with water that has glue, motor oil, or fingernail polish remover in it. Keep watering for a few weeks. What happens?

DID YOU KNOW?

The roots of plants wrap around soil and keep it from washing away in rainstorms. If you kill the plants, rain will carry the soil into rivers and ponds and new plants will find it difficult or impossible to grow.

I CAN... PROTECT A BODY OF WATER

WHAT CAN YOU DO?

The deep, blue ocean. A silvery lake. A frog-filled pond. A mighty river. A gurgling stream. You expect these bodies of water to be beautiful and clean and teeming with animals, right? You expect them to be good for swimming, boating, and fishing, correct? Unfortunately, many of them have become badly polluted.

▲ Never dump or throw anything into a body of water or on the land around it.
▲ Be careful of the plants around the edges of the water. Their roots help to keep soil from washing into the water during rain storms.
▲ If you find litter, pick it up and throw it in a trash can.

A WORD ABOUT WETLANDS

Swamps, marshes, and bogs are all wet places, or wetlands. They need protecting, too. Why?

▲ They provide homes for many animals and plants.
▲ Waterfowl use wetlands as feeding and resting areas during migration.
▲ People can catch fish and shellfish in wetlands.
▲ Visitors to wetlands can go boating, fishing, and nature-watching.

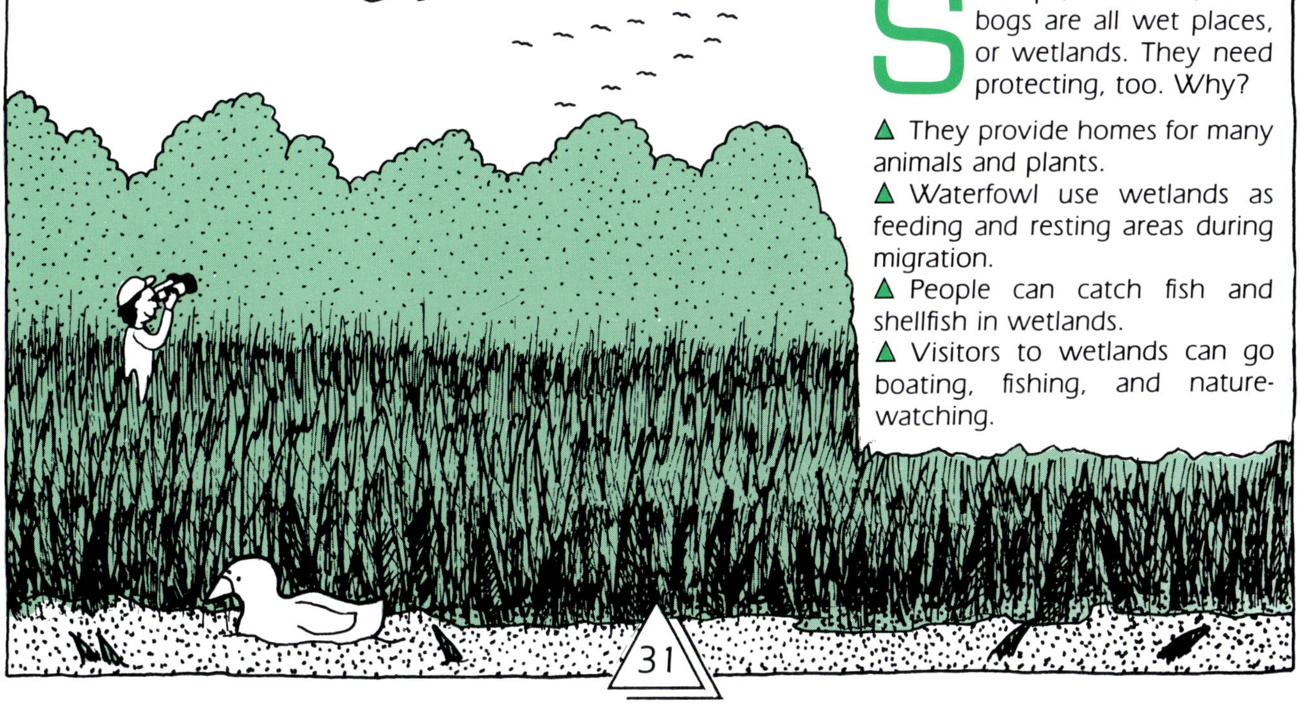

CHECK IT OUT

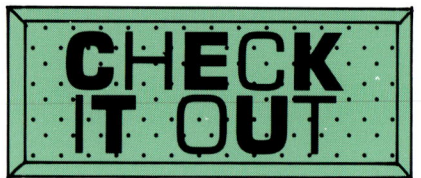

Choose a body of water or a wetland that is near you. Visit it often and learn all about it. Bring along a camera or sketch pad to "capture" the different plants and animals that live there. Keep your pictures in a scrapbook. Share your scrapbook with others.

DID YOU KNOW?

Many ocean fish and shellfish lay their eggs in the WETLANDS along the ocean. Their young hatch, grow up in the wetlands, and swim out to sea when they get big.

WHAT'S THE DIFFERENCE?

△ Several gallons of water can flow out of a faucet in a minute. If you leave the water running while you brush your teeth, you could use two or more gallons of water. Suppose you brush your teeth three times a day every day of the year. In a year's time, that could add up to 2,190 gallons of water. Here's how.

    2 gallons of water
    × 3 brushings
    × 365 days a year
    = 2,190 gallons of water

But suppose you run the water only long enough to wet the brush and then shut off the faucet. Then you could use as little as two cups of water at each brushing. That's only a small part of a gallon and quite a big savings.

    2 cups of water
    × 3 brushings
    × 365 days a year
    = 2,190 cups, or about 112 gallons, of water

Look: You've saved 2,078 gallons of water! Wasn't that easy?

△ The water that comes into your home is fresh and safe to drink. When you let perfectly clean water run down the drain to mix with used, dirty water, you are wasting water. Water that goes down the drain is no longer clean. Fresh water is too precious to waste in this way.

△ One out of every ten lakes, streams, and rivers in the United States is polluted with toxic (very poisonous) chemicals and metals. Household products cause some pollution. More pollution is caused by factories dumping chemicals. Other chemicals have seeped into the water from bug sprays farmers use. Polluted bodies of water cannot support many living things.

CHAPTER 4
FOR LAND AND RESOURCES

Caroline Duncan
New York, New York

Help! There's a monster on the rampage! This monster eats up the earth's resources. Then it spits them out all over the land. Do you know the name of this monster? It is You-Me-All-of-Us. You-Me-All-of-Us is greedy and careless and wasteful. And that creates a big trash and resource problem for the earth. In some places You-Me-All-of-Us creates huge mountains of garbage. In Staten Island, New York, You-Me-All-of-Us has made a pile of trash that rises 130 feet high. This "mountain" is the highest human-made point on the eastern seaboard. It spreads out over 3,000 acres.

In other places, You-Me-All-of-Us digs huge, craterlike holes. Why? The greedy monster wants the natural resources that are buried in the earth. It gobbles up coal and iron ore. It wants to use the resources for fuel and to manufacture things. In Wyoming, You-Me-All-of-Us created a 13,000-acre hole. That's about the size of 13,000 football fields.

Stop waste in its tracks. Don't waste earth's resources or add to its trash problem. Learn the facts about waste and what makes it. Then follow the earth-saving 3Rs:

▲ *Reduce* the amount of packaging and products you buy.
▲ *Reuse* as much—and as often—as possible.
▲ *Recycle* everything that you can.

Some tips on how to do this are in the next pages.

A WORD ABOUT RESOURCES

Look around you. Think about what you're wearing, what you're sitting on, what you're eating. Your surroundings are filled with things and products that people have made and grown. None of them would be possible without earth's natural resources.

Perhaps your shirt is made of organic cotton, a fabric made from a plant. Or your chair might be made from wood (from an oak tree) or plastic (from oil).

Maybe you're munching on popcorn (a crop) sprinkled with salt (a mineral).

Every person on earth uses natural resources. They are nature's gift to us. People in the United States use more than most. But sadly, much of what we use is thrown away soon after we buy it. Did you know that every person in the United States throws away about four pounds of trash every day? No wonder some people call the United States a "throwaway" society.

Wasting resources hurts the earth. For example, when too many trees are cut down, many animals lose their homes. The topsoil washes away, making it difficult for plants to grow. Without the trees and plants, there is less oxygen for us to breathe.

Wasting resources also causes another serious problem: trash heaps and litter. When we throw away things, we have to bury or burn them somewhere. Many American cities are running out of places to throw the trash.

DID YOU KNOW?

There is a special name for trash and garbage. It is called SOLID WASTE.

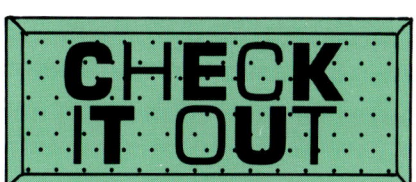

CHECK IT OUT

The average person living in the United States tosses away 28 pounds of trash each week. How do you measure up? Are you more or less wasteful? Do this to find out how much you throw away at home.

1. Get some trash bags, a scale, notepaper, and a pencil.
2. Each day collect the trash from all the trash baskets in the house.
3. Weigh what you collect. Write the amount on a chart like this.
4. At the end of the week, add up the amount.
5. Then divide this sum by the number of people in your family. The answer will be your share of the family's trash.
6. Now think about the other places where you create waste: at school, at church, at stores when you're shopping, at restaurants, in the car. How many more pounds a week do you think you are responsible for?

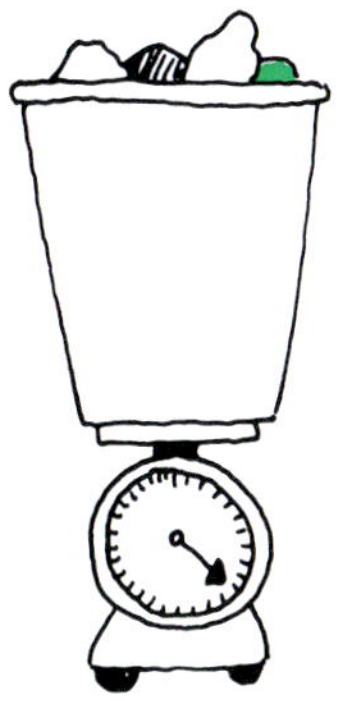

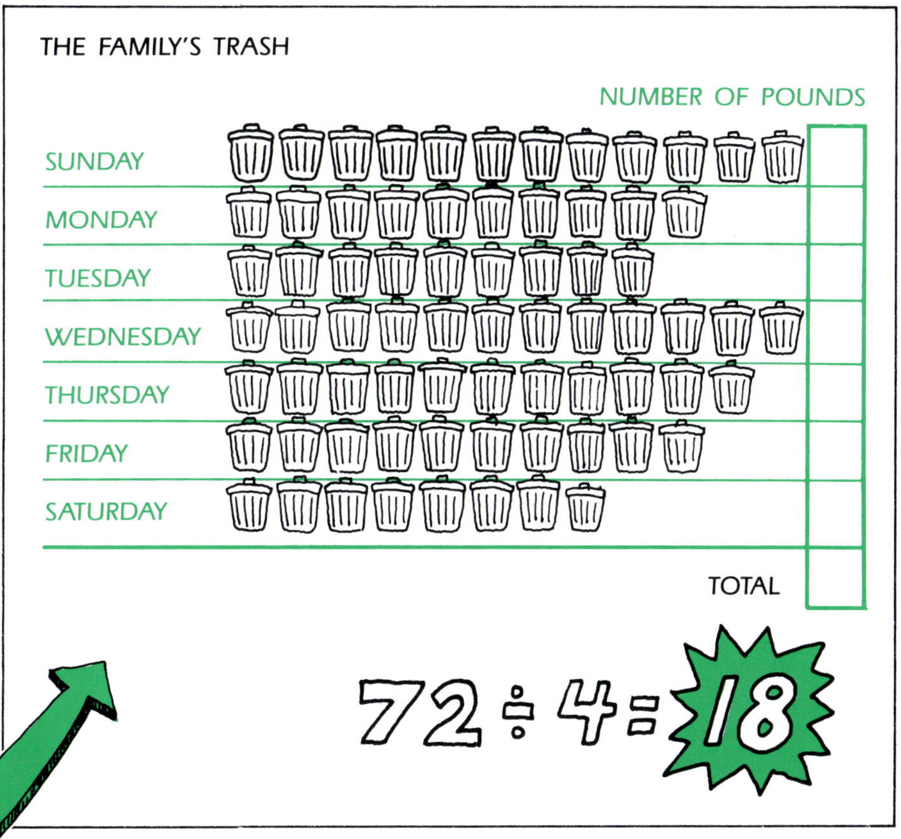

THE FAMILY'S TRASH

NUMBER OF POUNDS

SUNDAY	
MONDAY	
TUESDAY	
WEDNESDAY	
THURSDAY	
FRIDAY	
SATURDAY	
TOTAL	

$$72 \div 4 = 18$$

DID YOU KNOW?

Four out of 10 barrels of trash thrown away each day contain paper, $2\frac{1}{2}$ barrels contain plastic.

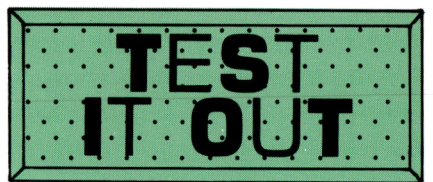
TEST IT OUT

Some things rot or decompose when left outside. The stuff they are made of finally becomes part of the earth again. We call these things biodegradable. Other things hardly change at all no matter how long they're left in the open. Sunshine, air, and water don't have much of an effect on them. They do not rot or become part of the earth again. And that means trouble for the environment—bigger and bigger trash heaps.

What things are biodegradable? Which aren't? Try this.

1. Get five or six jars with lids, water, some tape, and a marker.
2. Collect bits and pieces of some of the things you throw out every day: a potato chip, plastic wrap, facial tissue, aluminum foil, notebook paper, hair.
3. Half fill each jar with water.
4. Put a different throwaway sample in each jar.
5. Tape another bit of the throwaway to the outside of the jar.
6. Put the jars in a sunny place.
7. After a week, open the jars and examine the samples inside. Which changed the most? Did any start to rot and fall apart? Which hardly changed at all?

How do these samples compare to the samples taped outside the jar? What would happen if things we threw away never rotted or turned back into soil?

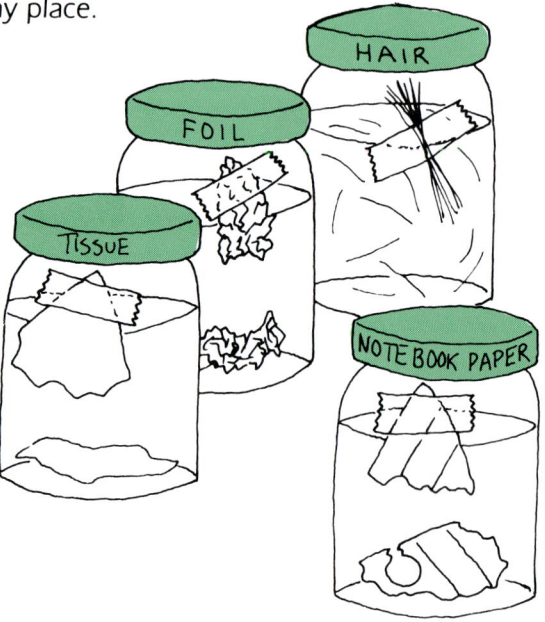

I CAN... BUY SMART

Has this happened to you? You buy a new toy or trinket. By the end of the day, it has fallen apart. Some things are just a waste of money. And that's bad enough. But poorly-made things also waste resources. It takes resources to make anything— but a well-made thing lasts. A poorly-made thing becomes trash very quickly.

DID YOU KNOW?

That aluminum can you throw away today will be here 500 years from now. Aluminum corrodes (wears away) very slowly.

ANSWER:

Animal and plant products decompose fairly quickly. Plastics and aluminum don't decompose even after hundreds of years. If animal and plant wastes lasted as long as plastics and aluminum, humans would have been buried in waste long ago!

WHAT CAN YOU DO?

▲ Make sure that what you buy is made to last. How can you tell? Examine it. Something made to last is made of sturdy materials. It is put together well.

▲ Look for the best buy for the money. Look at lots of toys. Compare quality. Compare prices. Pick the toy that looks like the best buy for the money. If you can't tell, get help from an adult.

▲ Beware of these bad buys: cheap plastic things (Cheap plastic is thin and brittle. Often it breaks very easily.), things sealed in a plastic bubble (It's hard to tell the quality of the item you're buying.), things displayed near checkout counters (Often these are cheaply made products arranged to grab your eye and your wallet.).

▲ Buy only what you need and no more.

TRY IT OUT

Think of items that kids buy by themselves: snacks, drinks, fast foods, toys, games. Read up on them in a consumer magazine like *Consumer Reports* or *Zillions,* the consumer magazine for kids. How are these products rated? Do they waste packaging? Then write your own buying guide for kids. Share it with your friends.

I CAN... TAKE CARE OF MY THINGS

What's wrong with this scene? Jill and Sandy are playing with their trucks in the backyard. Dad yells, "Dinner!" Jill and Sandy race for the house, leaving the trucks in the sandpile.

Things left outside soon get ruined. Metal parts get rusty. Plastic parts get brittle. Wood parts swell up and crack. Paint fades and peels. Soon nobody wants these toys and they get thrown away, cluttering up more landfills.

But if you take care of toys and other things, they can last for years and years.

DID YOU KNOW?

Three out of every 10 barrels of trash that go to the dump are from packaging.

WHAT CAN YOU DO?

▲ Put things away when you're not using them.
▲ Don't leave toys, bikes, skates, or tools outside overnight or in bad weather.
▲ Use things properly. Don't treat them rough.
▲ Keep things clean and in good repair.
▲ When things break, try to repair them right away. Keep a repair kit handy for small jobs. In it keep a few tools, all-purpose oil, and glue.

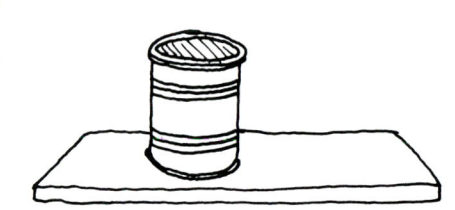

TEST IT OUT

What causes metals to rust? Try this out.

1. Get three tin soup cans. (Aluminum ones won't work.)
2. Bury one in the ground. Leave one outside in the open. Put one in a dry indoor spot.
3. Check the cans once or twice a week. Which ones rust? Which one rusts the fastest? Which doesn't rust at all? What's the explanation?

ANSWER:

Metals rust when air and water combine on the surface of the metal.

I CAN... SAY "NO" TO THROWAWAYS

Time for a trash check. Check out all the trash baskets in your house. How much of the stuff in them was used once and thrown away? How much was hardly used at all?

People in the United States buy throw-away products almost without thinking. We use things for only a short while—sometimes not even a minute. Then we throw them away. Why do we use throwaways? Throwing it all away is awfully wasteful.

WHAT CAN YOU DO?

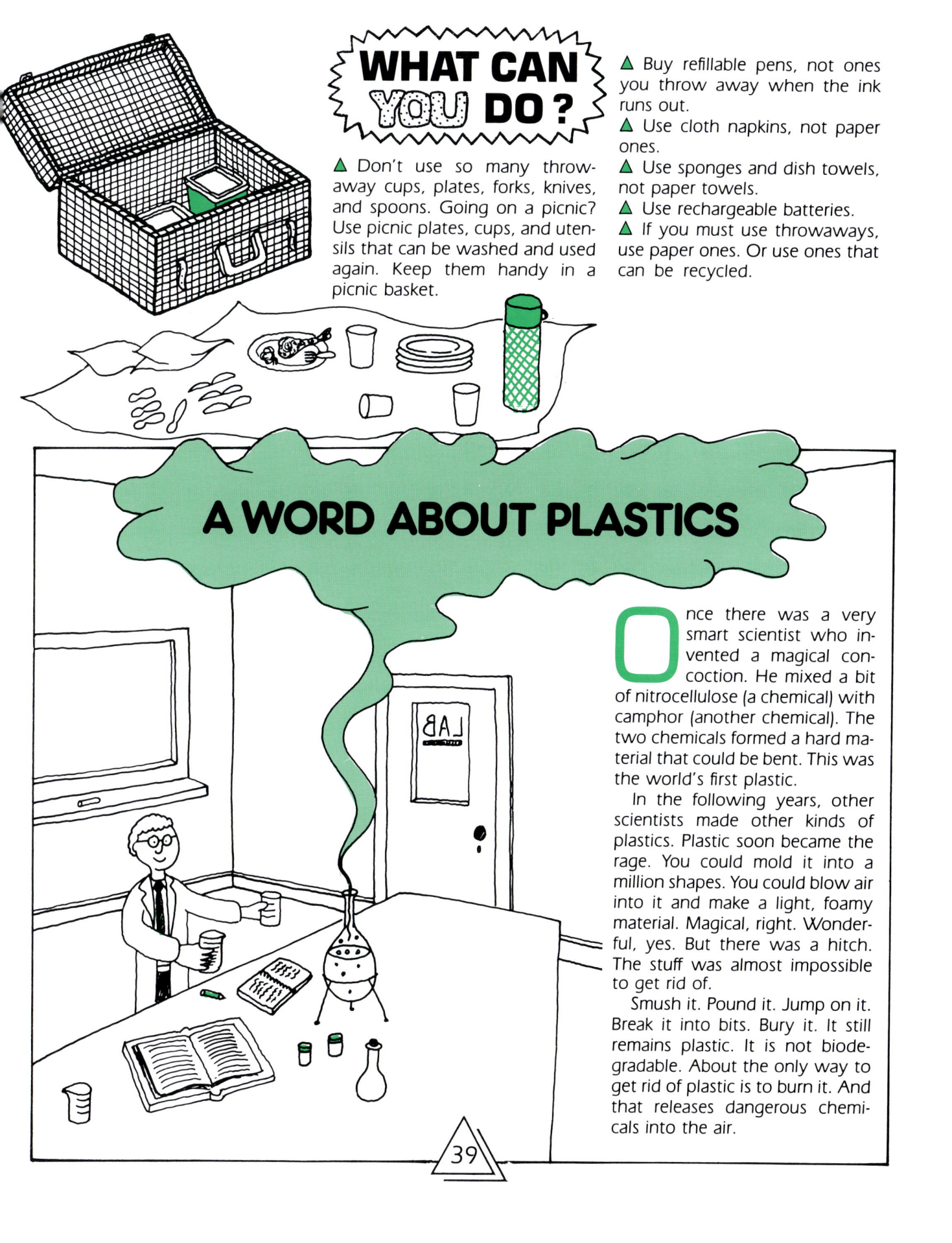

▲ Don't use so many throwaway cups, plates, forks, knives, and spoons. Going on a picnic? Use picnic plates, cups, and utensils that can be washed and used again. Keep them handy in a picnic basket.

▲ Buy refillable pens, not ones you throw away when the ink runs out.
▲ Use cloth napkins, not paper ones.
▲ Use sponges and dish towels, not paper towels.
▲ Use rechargeable batteries.
▲ If you must use throwaways, use paper ones. Or use ones that can be recycled.

A WORD ABOUT PLASTICS

Once there was a very smart scientist who invented a magical concoction. He mixed a bit of nitrocellulose (a chemical) with camphor (another chemical). The two chemicals formed a hard material that could be bent. This was the world's first plastic.

In the following years, other scientists made other kinds of plastics. Plastic soon became the rage. You could mold it into a million shapes. You could blow air into it and make a light, foamy material. Magical, right. Wonderful, yes. But there was a hitch. The stuff was almost impossible to get rid of.

Smush it. Pound it. Jump on it. Break it into bits. Bury it. It still remains plastic. It is not biodegradable. About the only way to get rid of plastic is to burn it. And that releases dangerous chemicals into the air.

TRY IT OUT

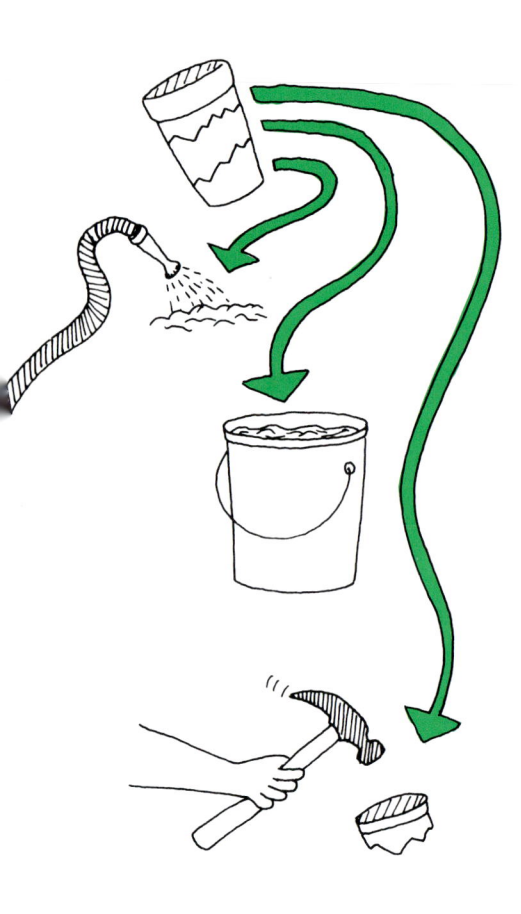

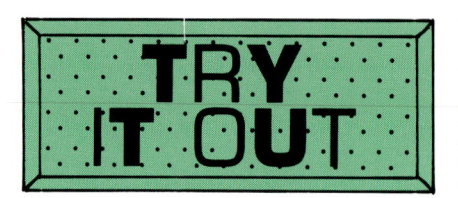

Can you get rid of plastic without burning it? Here's a test.

1. Get a plastic foam cup and divide it into three pieces.
2. Bury one piece under a few inches of soil and keep it moist. Put the second piece in a pail of water. Pound one piece with a hammer.
3. Check from time to time. Do you see any change? Does the foam begin to rot or become part of the earth again?
4. Do the same thing with a piece of paper cup. How do the materials compare? Which material can turn to basic elements? What helps to decompose paper? Does the same process help decay plastic?

I CAN... BE A PACKAGE BUSTER

A package is the throwaway of all throwaways. Its only purpose is to get something from one place to another. Then it gets tossed in the trash. The You-Me-All-of-Us monster really went crazy when it designed packages.

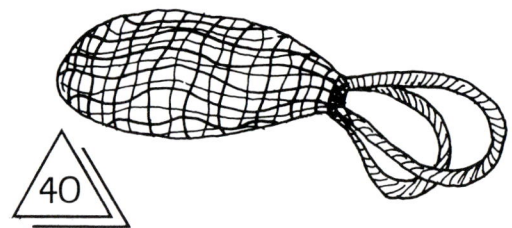

WHAT CAN YOU DO?

▲ Don't accept new paper and plastic bags from the store. Reuse an old shopping bag, or take a cloth or string carryall with you.
▲ Don't buy packs of single-serving products such as juice boxes or individual chips or cereal packages. The more divided up a package is, the more wasteful it is.
▲ Pass up things that are overpackaged—where there is twice as much of the packaging as there is of the thing you're buying.
▲ Buy reusable containers for storing food. Old glass jars make good food savers.
▲ Carry your lunch in a lunch box instead of a paper bag. Use a Thermos-type bottle for drinks instead of throwaway containers. Put your sandwich in a reusable plastic container instead of a sandwich bag.
▲ When you wrap things yourself, be thrifty. Use only as much as you need.

TEST IT OUT

Is a large package less wasteful than a bunch of small ones? Try this.

1. Unwrap a loaf of bread. Measure the size of the package it comes in.
2. Now wrap each slice of bread in waxed paper or plastic wrap. Measure the amount you used.
3. Compare the two amounts. Which method of packaging is the most wasteful?

ANSWER:

It takes a 290 sq. in. piece of plastic to cover a 16 oz. loaf of bread. To cover one slice of bread takes a piece about 9" square, or 81 sq. inches. To wrap 18 slices would take 1,498 sq. inches.

I CAN... REUSE THROWAWAYS

Hold on there! What's that you're about to throw away? Before you do it, think. Could it be used a second time? Is there something else you could use it for? Could someone else use it? Many things we throw out can really be used over and over again—reused or recycled in new ways.

WHAT CAN YOU DO?

▲ Hang on to that aluminum foil. If you wash it and fold it neatly, it can be used over and over again. Plastic bags can be washed and saved too.

▲ Don't throw away jars and plastic containers that food comes in. Wash them well. Then use them again to store food or small items.

▲ Wash out and store those milk and juice cartons. They can be used later in many ways. Cut them down and plant seeds in them. Or use them to make bird feeders.

▲ Don't toss that frozen orange juice container. Use it for growing seeds and cuttings. Or wrap it in colorful paper and twine and use it for a pencil holder.

▲ Plastic foam (polystyrene) cups last almost forever. Scientists say they may last 1,000 years. So why not make something long-lasting out of them? Save them and use them to make Christmas decorations or an interesting sculpture. All it takes is a little imagination.

TRY IT OUT

How long can you keep the same piece of foil in use? Why not keep a mini-diary to find out? Start with the day you "adopt" the foil (the day you bring it home from the store). Then note each time you use it and how. When the foil can no longer be used, give it a proper burial—in your aluminum recycling bin.

I CAN... RECYCLE CANS, GLASS, PAPER, AND CARDBOARD

Here are some fascinating facts about trash. Each year we throw away more than:

△ 1 million tons of aluminum cans and foil
△ 35 billion aluminum cans
△ $36\frac{1}{2}$ billion steel cans
△ 11 million tons of glass, mostly bottles and jars
△ 60 million tons of paper and paperboard
△ 10 million tons of newspaper
△ $4\frac{1}{2}$ million tons of office paper
△ 12 million tons of metal
△ 10 million tons of plastic
△ 12 million tons of rubber, leather, textiles, and wood
△ 12 million tons of food waste
△ 28 million tons of yard waste
△ $1\frac{1}{2}$ billion pens
△ 2 billion razors and blades
△ 16 billion diapers

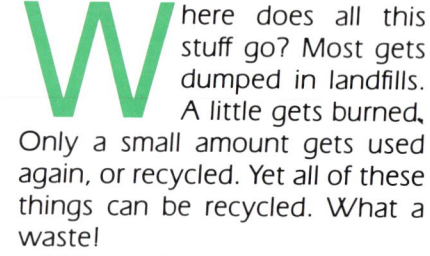

Where does all this stuff go? Most gets dumped in landfills. A little gets burned. Only a small amount gets used again, or recycled. Yet all of these things can be recycled. What a waste!

When things are recycled, they are ground and melted down or mushed up. Then they are used over again. Recycling saves resources. It also saves energy. Why?

To make something out of anything takes energy. But it doesn't take as much energy to make things from recycled materials as it does from raw materials. Take aluminum cans, for instance. To make an aluminum can from scratch, you first have to get minerals out of the ground. This takes energy. Then you need to turn the minerals into aluminum. This takes energy. Then you need to turn the aluminum into a can. This takes more energy. But if you make the can from recycled aluminum, you can skip the first two steps.

WHAT CAN YOU DO?

▲ Find out what materials your community recycles.

▲ Set up a place in your home to collect and sort them.

▲ Carry the things out to the curb on recycling day; or with your parents, visit the recycling center in your community.

▲ Buy products that can be recycled. Look for this recycling symbol—three arrows in a circle.

▲ Buy products whose boxes are made from recycled paper materials. How to tell? You will see a recycled symbol, and the inside of the box will be gray or tan in color.

TRY IT OUT

There are lots of trash organizers on the market, but you can design your own. Here's one idea.

1. Get six or seven plastic cans, cardboard boxes, or even brown paper bags.

2. Label them like this: glass, steel, aluminum, plastic, newspaper, white paper, mixed paper (or whatever categories your community recycles).

3. Put them in a corner of your house—and use them to sort your trash.

A WORD ABOUT GARBAGE

Here's a magical mixture plants love. And it's a good way to recycle garbage and garden scraps.

1. Take a bunch of kitchen scraps: coffee grounds, paper towels, vegetable and fruit peels, eggshells, leftover bread, pasta, cake, cookies, and the like. (Don't use greasy things or meat or dairy products.)

2. Mix with lawn and garden wastes such as grass clippings, weeds, dead flowers, and leaves.

3. Top with a little manure and soil.

4. Moisten with water and let it "cook" in the sun. Turn or mix the pile—about once a month during warm weather. In a few months you'll have a rich "bio-stew" for plants. Gardeners call it compost.

I CAN... HAND DOWN THINGS

When you're a kid, you often outgrow clothes quickly—even before they're worn out. So what do you do with them: throw them out? Never—that's wasteful. A great idea is to hand them down—give them to someone else to use. There are other things too that people often throw out—perfectly good things that someone else could use. Toys, bikes, blankets, curtains, furniture, books, tools, jewelry, purses, boots, and belts are all items that can be given away.

WHAT CAN YOU DO?

▲ Think first of relatives or friends. Younger brothers and sisters might appreciate receiving your worn-in jeans.

▲ Give used things to a hospital thrift shop, the Salvation Army, or Goodwill Industries. These groups are usually glad to get the things you're passing on—if they're clean and in good condition. They sell these items inexpensively in their stores, and then give the money they make to charity.

▲ Take your old things to a second-time-around shop. When your stuff is sold, they give you a small part of the profit.

▲ Give used toys, books, and games to hospitals. They'll cheer up young patients.

▲ Hold a tag or yard sale to get rid of old things. Tag sales are fun and you'll make a little money.

DID YOU KNOW?

Seven out of 10 pails of garbage can be made into COMPOST. Yet less than 1 out of 10 pails of garbage goes into the compost heap.

TRY IT OUT

Want to hold a tag sale? Here are some tips. But be sure to get an adult's permission or a permit from your community.

1. Go through your things and decide what you want to sell.
2. Dust, wash, and polish everything. Make the items look as good as you can.
3. Put price tags on each thing. Be reasonable. Used things should cost a lot less than new things.
4. Set up tables in the garage, or along the driveway, or in the front of your house.
5. Arrange everything neatly on the tables.
6. Have a cash box for making change. Start out with at least five dollars in bills and coins.
7. Get a friend to help you. Perhaps you can pool your things together. You do the selling. Your friend handles the money. Or vice versa.
8. Early on the day of the sale, put up signs around the neighborhood.

Tag Sale
SATURDAY 9:00 to 3:00

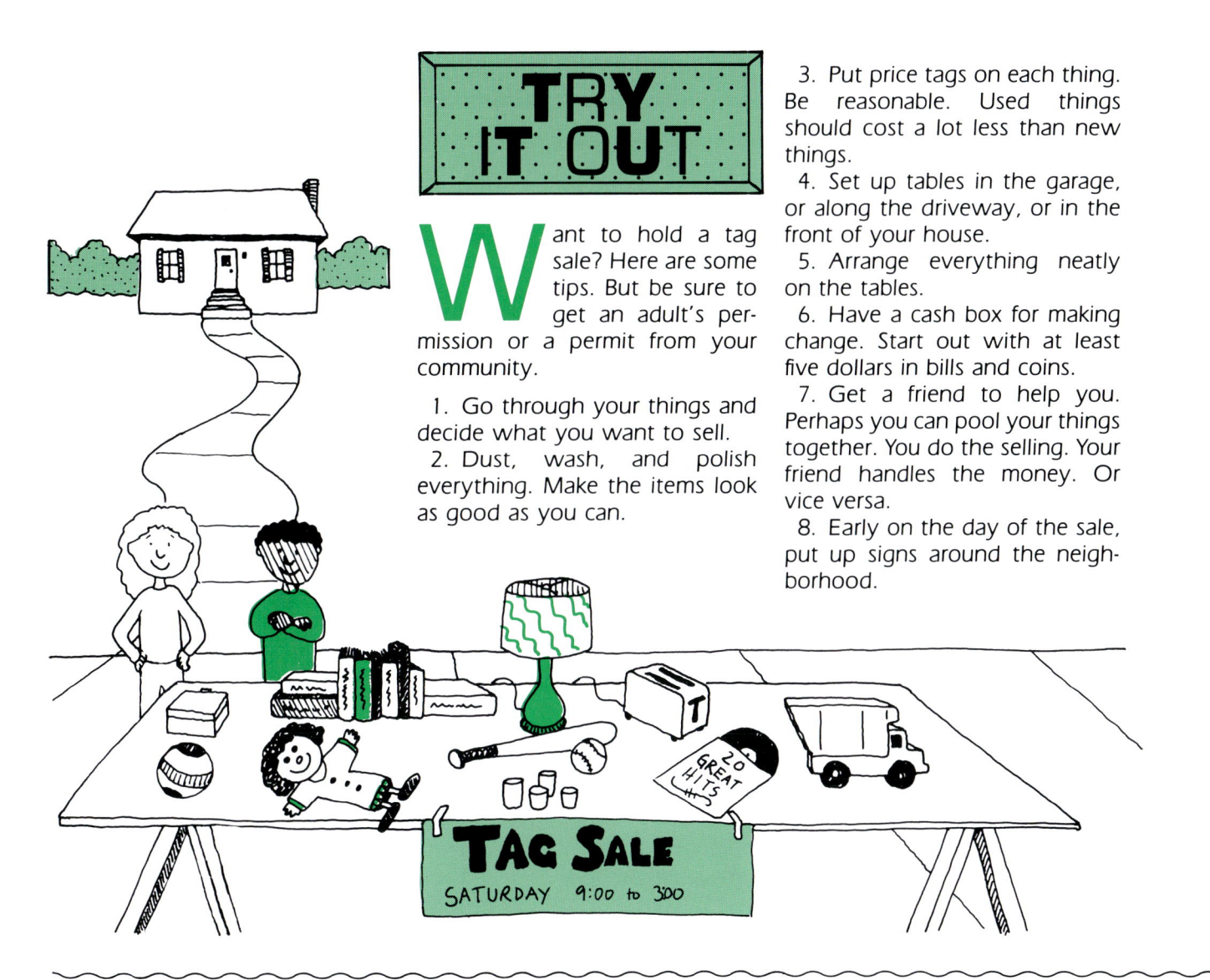

WHAT'S THE DIFFERENCE?

▲ Good news! When you buy smart, you save money. You also save resources, make less trash, save space on earth, save energy, and make less pollution.
▲ When you say "no" to throwaways and extra packages, you do all of the above.
▲ When you take care of things, you do all of the above.
▲ When you recycle, you do all of the above.

CHAPTER 5
FOR PLANTS AND PLACES

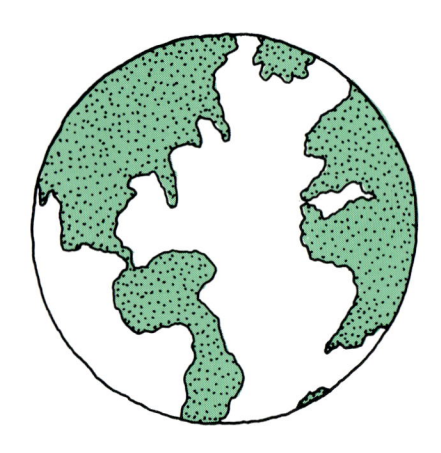

Earth is a fascinating planet. It is full of opposites. There are mountains and flatlands, highlands and lowlands, wetlands and drylands, forests and grasslands. Each of these places is special in its own way. Each contains its own unique soil, plants, animals, and climate.

Once most of the places on earth were quite wild. There weren't very many people then to build cities, highways, factories, and farms. Wild animals and wild plants had much of the earth to themselves.

Now there are more than five billion people on earth. People have taken over and changed most of the wild places. It's more difficult to find places where wild plants and animals can grow freely and undisturbed.

Many people are concerned about this problem. They want to protect the places where wild plants grow—whether it's a mountain or our own backyards. And they want to protect the forests, jungles, and other special places, or habitats, where wild animals make their homes.

DID YOU KNOW?

There are 350,000 different kinds of plants on earth. About 250,000 of these produce flowers.

WHAT CAN YOU DO?

You can visit your library to learn about wild places and what is threatening them. There are many books, articles, films, and TV programs that explain the problems and possible solutions. Once you know how, you can help protect all places—wild or not—where plants and animals live.

A WORD ABOUT PARKS AND WILDERNESS AREAS

We in the United States are lucky to have many national parks, seashores, lakeshores, and rivers. We also have many wilderness areas. In such places land, plants, and animals are protected. People can't build or do any other activity that will disturb the plants and animals. These very special places belong to all of us. It is up to all of us to protect and care for them.

OUR MOST POPULAR NATIONAL PARKS AND SEASHORES

PARK	WHERE IT IS	WHAT'S SPECIAL ABOUT IT
Cape Cod National Seashore	Massachusetts	Windswept beaches, marshes, and bays
Cape Hatteras National Seashore	North Carolina	Windswept beaches, marshes, and bays
Everglades National Park	Florida	Grassy wetlands and mangrove swamps
Glacier National Park	Montana	Mountains, lakes, and glaciers
Grand Canyon National Park	Arizona	Deep, majestic canyons and a mighty river
Grand Teton National Park	Wyoming	Snowcapped mountains
Great Smoky Mountain National Park	North Carolina and Tennessee	Green mountains with lots of trees
King's Canyon National Park	California	Deep canyons, high mountains, giant sequoia trees
Olympic National Park	Washington	Cool rain forest, beautiful mountains
Rocky Mountain National Park	Colorado	Jagged, rocky mountains, forests
Sequoia National Park	California	Giant sequoia trees, high mountains
Shenandoah National Park	Virginia	Tree-covered mountains
Yellowstone National Park	Idaho, Montana, and Wyoming	Canyons, waterfalls, and giant geysers
Yosemite National Park	California	Mountains, waterfalls, giant sequoia trees

TRY IT OUT

Choose a national park or seashore that you would like to visit, and plan an imaginary trip. (Who knows, it could become a real journey in the future!) Send away for literature to find out about the climate, what to pack, where to stay, and what plants and animals you might be lucky enough to see. Or read about the place in a magazine or book.

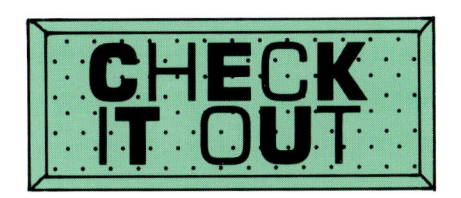

DID YOU KNOW?

There are many different kinds of soil on earth. Some are sandy. Some are rocky. Some are full of clay. Some have lots of dead plants (compost) in them. Among the best soils in the world are in the center of the United States. In some grassy places, the soil is 3 to 4 feet thick and very fertile.

CHECK IT OUT

What kinds of wild plants grow where you live? Take a nature walk to find out. Then make a record of what you find. Here's one way.

1. Collect leaves from the common trees and shrubs that grow around you. Also collect leaves from smaller plants. In some places the only wild plants are weeds, but some of these are very pretty and interesting.
2. Place the leaves between sections of newspaper.
3. Place heavy books on the sections.
4. When the leaves dry out (in about two weeks), gently remove them.
5. Paste them on a poster or in a scrapbook and write their names under them.

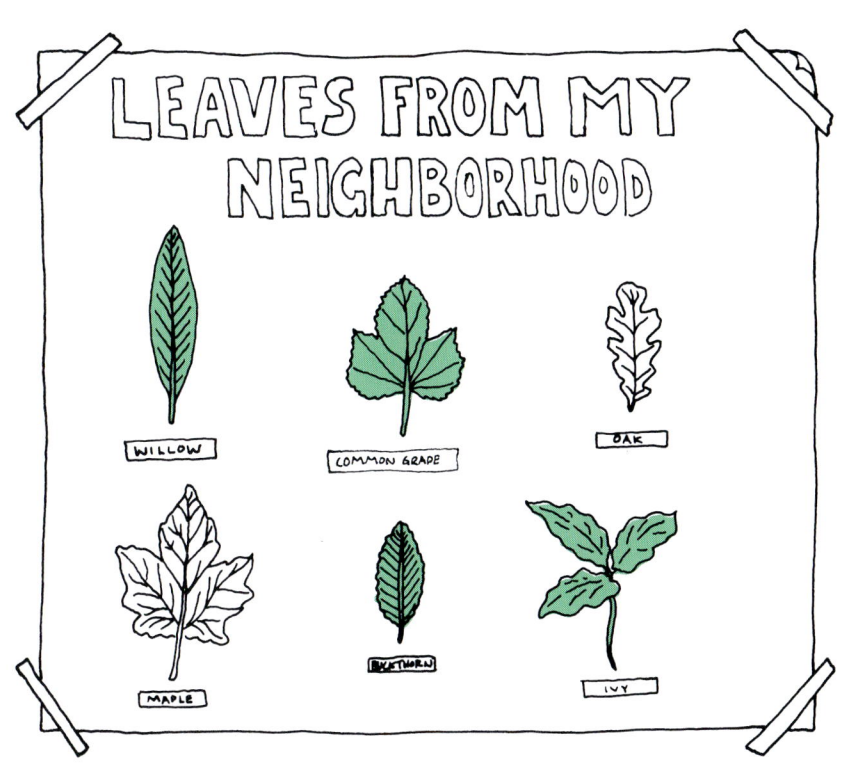

Caution: Don't pick leaves from poisonous or very rare or protected plants. Get a book and an adult to help you identify the plants.

LEAVES FROM MY NEIGHBORHOOD

- WILLOW
- COMMON GRAPE
- OAK
- MAPLE
- BUCKTHORN
- IVY

DID YOU KNOW?

The world can be divided into 10 to 15 main climate zones. The warmest zones are in the center of the world about halfway between the North Pole and the South Pole. The coldest zones are at the North and South poles.

I CAN...
BE A FRIEND TO TREES (AND OTHER PLANTS)

Get out your shovel and join the party. All across the country people are planting trees. One group has planted 100,000,000 of them—that's 100 times a million! Why are people planting trees?

Trees are terrific.

Trees . . .
- put oxygen into the air.
- give homes to birds and other animals.
- offer shade.
- release moisture into the air and keep it cool.
- send roots into the ground that keep soil from washing away when it rains.

Trees also give us a variety of special things:
- fruits and nuts and syrups
- wood
- paper
- rubber
- cellophane
- felt
- turpentine, pitch, resin, lacquer, wood alcohol
- medicines

It's hard to imagine a world without trees. Yet the world is losing them at a fast rate. People are chopping down trees faster than new ones can grow. Some are cut down for wood. Others are cut down to make paper and cardboard. Still others are cut down to make room for farms and cattle ranches, highways, cities, and shopping malls.

DID YOU KNOW?

The roots of a tree spread out about as far as the branches of the tree do.

DID YOU KNOW?

A forest can last forever if it is taken care of. You can even cut down trees within a forest and still not harm the forest . . . if you don't cut down too many. Why? New trees grow back.

50

WHAT CAN YOU DO?

▲ Plant a tree in your yard. No yard? Then get others to help you plant trees at school or in the neighborhood.

▲ Plant other green things too —inside and outside your home. All plants, even grass, take harmful gases out of the air and replace them with life-giving oxygen.

▲ Don't harm trees. Don't break their branches. Don't cut them down. Don't carve your name in their bark. Be especially careful around saplings, very young trees.

▲ Be careful with matches. Never make a fire in very dry woods or without an adult's help.

▲ To find out about other ways to be a friend to trees, write to:

Tree Amigos
Center for Environment Study
143 Bostwick NE
Grand Rapids, MI 49503

▲ Don't waste wood, paper, cardboard, and other products made from trees.

A WORD ABOUT CHRISTMAS TREES

Each year we cut down millions of trees for the holidays. When the holidays are over, we throw away the trees. What a waste!

But there is something else you can do. You can buy a live tree instead of a cut one. Live trees are about twice as expensive as cut ones. But when the holidays are over, you can plant them. That way, you'll have a tree forever.

DID YOU KNOW?

Thousands of trees are killed each year by careless drivers of dirt bikes and other all-terrain vehicles. Many of these bikes are driven by kids.

TRY IT OUT

Can you grow a tree from seeds? Give it a try!

1. Collect seeds from a tree in your neighborhood.
2. Put the seeds in a pot.
3. Set the pot of seeds in a sunny window, water it often, and watch the seeds sprout and grow.
4. After a few weeks, pull out all but the healthiest sprout.
5. When your young tree is about a year old or a few inches high, plant it in the ground. To protect it, put a little fence around it.

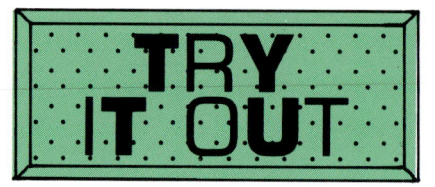

TRY IT OUT

Here are some tips on planting a tree.

1. Choose a healthy tree, five to six feet tall. Visit your local nursery, or landscape or gardening center for advice.
2. Select a sunny place to plant it. The place shouldn't be rocky or full of roots.
3. Cultivate or till a patch of soil. It should be as deep as the tree's root ball and at least three times its diameter.
4. Dig a hole in the middle of the spot just slightly deeper than the root ball.
5. Put some compost in the hole.
6. Set the root ball in the hole and cover with soil.
7. Water the tree well to settle the soil and remove air pockets.
8. Spread two to three inches of mulch over the planting area.
9. Water the tree every few days until it is growing well. Then water only during long dry spells.

READ IT OUT

Learn a poem about a tree. Then recite it to your friends and family.

DID YOU KNOW?

A clump of trees can cool the air by several degrees.

CITY TREES

The trees along this city street,
   Save for the traffic and the trains,
Would make a sound as thin and sweet
   As trees in country lanes.

And people standing in their shade
   Out of a shower, undoubtedly
Would hear such music as is made
   Upon a country tree.

Oh, little leaves that are so dumb
   Against the shrieking city air,
I watch you when the wind has come, —
   I know what sound is there.

Edna St. Vincent Millay

I CAN... BE A PAPER "SCROOGE"

Do you know where paper comes from? It comes from trees. Millions of trees are cut down each year to make paper. Most of these trees are grown on tree farms. Nevertheless, making paper from trees can be a wasteful process. And it creates air and water pollution besides. That's a good reason to save paper.

DID YOU KNOW?

At one time, forests covered 15 billion acres of the earth's surface. Today only 10 billion acres of the earth are forested. And we are losing forests at the rate of more than 98,000 acres a day.

WHAT CAN YOU DO?

▲ Don't use paper bags to carry groceries. Do what the kids in Petaluma, California, do instead. They use "earth bags" made of canvas. These can be used over and over again. See their design for an earth bag on this page.

▲ Write on both sides of your paper.

▲ Share magazines, books, and newspapers with friends.

▲ Use cloth napkins instead of paper ones.

▲ Use a sponge or dishcloth instead of paper towels.

▲ Don't waste toilet paper and facial tissues.

▲ Carry a lunch box instead of bagging your lunch.

▲ Buy recycled paper. Look for a label like this.

CARTON MADE FROM 100% RECYCLED PAPERBOARD MINIMUM 35% POST-CONSUMER CONTENT

▲ Recycle paper yourself.

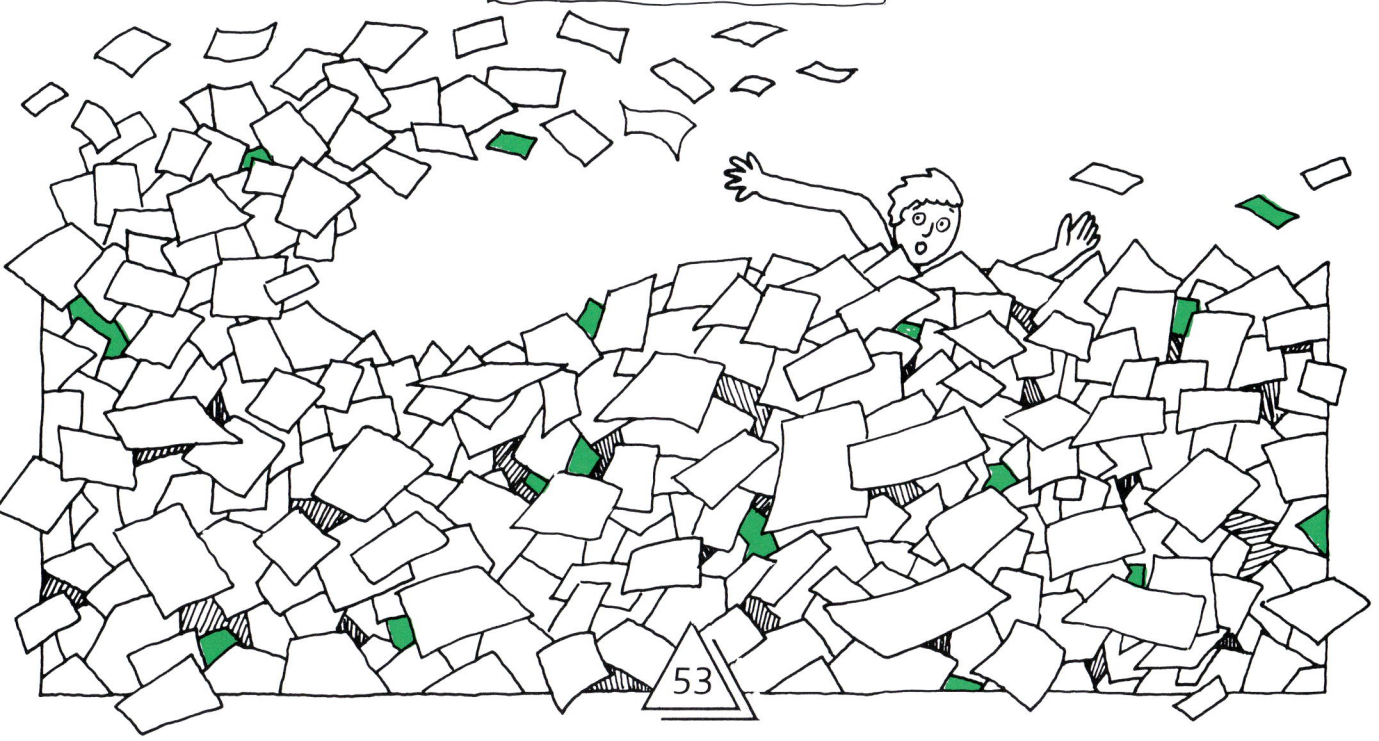

A WORD ABOUT GIFT WRAPPING

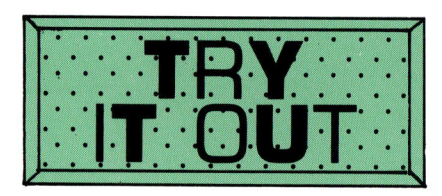

We love to wrap gifts in fancy packages. An enormous amount of paper and ribbon gets used this way. You can cut down on package waste by reusing gift wraps. You can also invent new ways to wrap gifts that aren't so wasteful. Newspaper—especially colorful comics—makes a good gift wrap. So do those pretty bags you get at department stores. Always think of ways to reuse paper. You can reuse ribbons and gift boxes too—over and over again.

TRY IT OUT

Here's a way you can recycle newspapers—make newspaper logs. Newspaper logs burn almost as hotly as wood but not as long. Make some logs for your own family. Or give them as gifts. It takes about ten newspaper sections to make one log.

1. Get a stack of newspapers, twine, scissors, a 2½-foot dowel or narrow stick.
2. Separate the newspapers into sections. (Don't use any colored or glossy sections, such as the magazine section.)
3. Place a newspaper section before you.
4. Put the dowel at the bottom of the paper.
5. Tightly roll all but three inches of the paper around the dowel.
6. Slide a second newspaper section over the end of the first one.
7. Repeat steps 5 and 6 until you have a thick log.
8. Tie the log with twine and pull out the dowel.

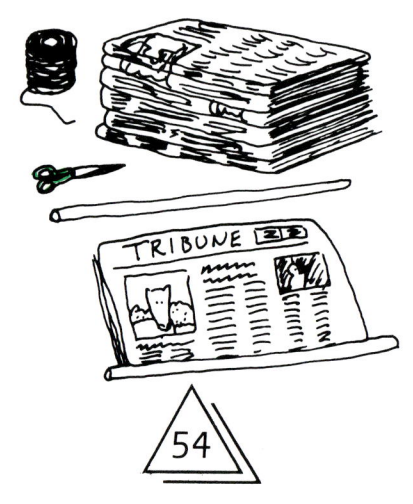

DID YOU KNOW?

Each time you use a piece of paper, you are using a little bit of a tree. Trees are cut down and sent to a paper mill. There they are ground up and mixed with chemicals. Finally, they are rolled out into paper.

54

I CAN... LEAVE WILD FLOWERS ALONE

Did you know that some flowers will grow only in very special places? They need a certain kind of soil, a certain amount of rain, and a certain amount of shade or sun. If you change any one of these things, the flowers can't grow. In the United States, about 200 of our wild flowers and other plants are in danger of dying out. Why? Because people are changing the wild places these plants need to live.

WHAT CAN YOU DO?

▲ Learn about the wild flowers and plants around you. Find out which are rare and in danger.
▲ Don't pick rare wild flowers. Pick only flowers from your garden or flowers that you know grow in great numbers. If you don't know for sure, leave the flowers alone.

DID YOU KNOW?

We use nearly half the world's newsprint (newspaper paper). We throw away more than 4 million tons of office paper and nearly 10 million tons of newspapers each year. One out of every 4 barrels of city trash is paper.

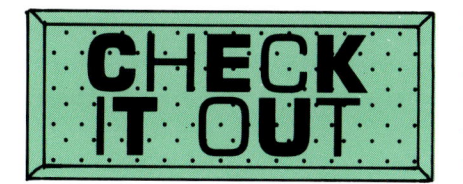

CHECK IT OUT

Did you know that flowers are a most important plant part? Flowers produce seeds from which new plants grow. To check it out, do this.

1. Pick one or two flowers from your garden. Faded flowers are best for finding seeds.
2. Find the bulbous part of the flower, called the pistil. In some flowers, it is underneath the petals. In others it is inside the petals.
3. Get an adult to help you cut the pistil in half. You may find little seeds forming inside the pistil. If they are very small, you may need a magnifying glass to see them.

DO YOU KNOW?

Green plants have little holes under their leaves. Through these holes they take in carbon dioxide from the air. Carbon dioxide is a combination of carbon and oxygen. Plants use the carbon from carbon dioxide to make their own food. Then they send the unused oxygen out into the air through the holes in their leaves.

A WORD ABOUT RARE PLANTS

Want to protect all of earth's rare plants? Don't take or buy any plants from the wild. Make sure all the plants you buy are grown in nurseries. Plants to beware of are desert plants and tropical forest plants.

"My mother took my two brothers and me to a forest near our house. She showed us some wild flowers called *pink lady's slippers* growing there. They were very beautiful. My mother told us never to pick them because they are very rare. She had first found some growing there when she was a teenager. There were only three then, but now there are at least 40! She checks on them every year.

"I really enjoyed seeing the lady's slippers. I wish that every person could have that experience. It was super!"

Lydia Souders of Hustontown, Pennsylvania, wrote this letter to *Ranger Rick* magazine.

pink lady's slipper

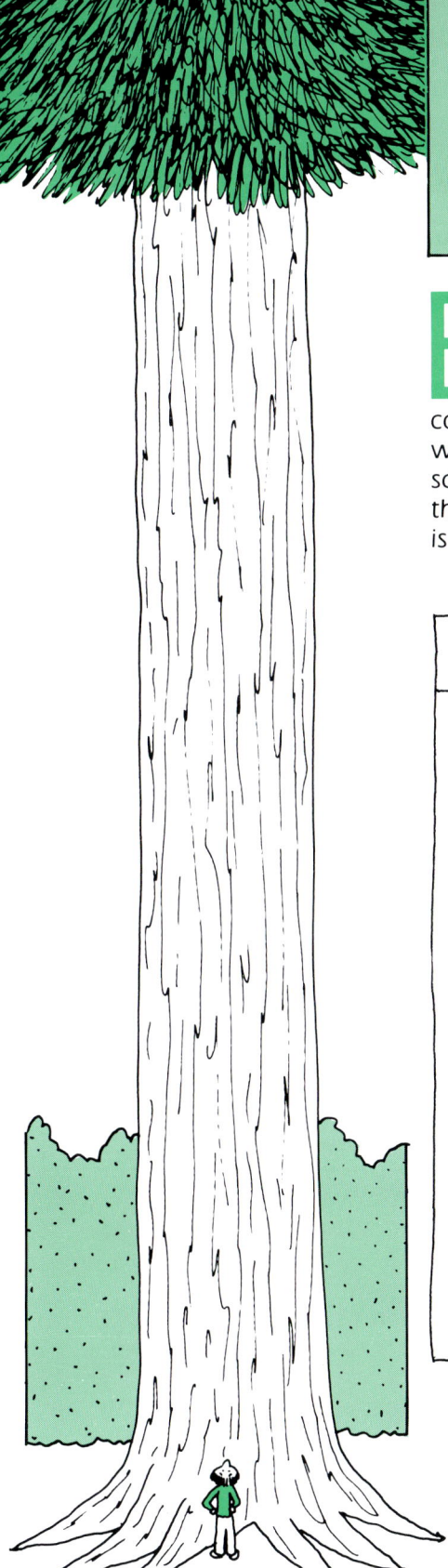

I CAN... PROTECT WILD PLACES

Each year millions of acres of land change from wild to not wild. If something isn't done, one day our country will have few—or no—wild places. The chart shows some places in the United States that are in great danger and what is endangering them:

IN DANGER	WHERE	WHY
Sequoia forests	California	Tree cutting
Redwood forests	California	Tree cutting
Northern forests	Northern United States	Tree cutting; farming; building
Wetlands	Everywhere	Building; farming; pollution
Islands and coastlines	Everywhere	Building
Arctic tundra	Alaska	Oil drilling
Western forests	Western United States	Tree cutting; ranching; fires
Wild rivers	Throughout the United States	Dams; pollution
National parks	Throughout the United States	Too many visitors; carelessness; pollution; fires

DID YOU KNOW?

Every year, 40 to 50 million acres of tropical forest are cut down or burned. That's an area about the size of Washington State.

WHAT CAN YOU DO?

▲ Join groups that work to save wild places. Read their newsletters to find out what people are doing to help.

▲ Treat all wild places as if they were parks. Here's a good rule to follow:

TAKE NOTHING BUT PICTURES... LEAVE NOTHING BUT FOOTSTEPS

FIND IT OUT

Would you like to know more about America's parks and wild lands? Write to:

Department of Interior
19th and C Streets N.W.
Washington, D.C. 20240

DID YOU KNOW?

Scientists figured out how many types of plants and animals lived in one section of rain forest about half the size of the city of San Francisco. They found 545 kinds of birds, 100 kinds of dragonflies, and 792 kinds of butterflies.

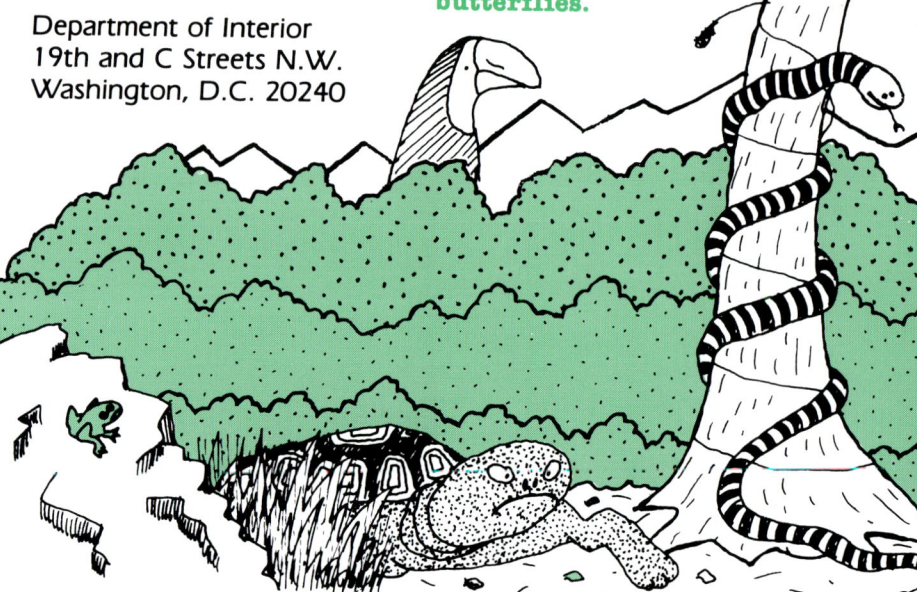

I CAN... STAND UP FOR TROPICAL RAIN FORESTS

What's so special about a rain forest? It's green, it's damp, and it's full of fascinating animals and plants. Think of any exotic or unusual animal you've seen in zoos, books, or films. Chances are it makes its home in the rain forest. Think of your favorite tropical houseplant. Chances are it too lives in the rain forest. Tropical rain forests are home to more than half the world's plants and half the world's animals.

If you visited a tropical rain forest, you might find parrots and monkeys chattering in treetops, giant snakes wrapped around branches, fern-lined streams, magnificent sky-scraping trees, slinking cats, darting hummingbirds, and brilliant flowers.

Tropical rain forests, which are found in the warm middle parts of the world, are big oxygen makers. The plants that grow there give the world nearly half its oxygen. These plants also use up much of the world's carbon dioxide.

Rain forests also give us lots of foods: bananas, sugar, cinnamon, cocoa, cashews, pineapples, and papayas. Their trees give us rubber and beautiful hardwoods such as mahogany, teak, and rosewood. Most importantly, each year many medicines are discovered from the plants that grow in tropical rain forests.

You'd think that people would work very hard to protect rain forests. But this hasn't happened. Instead, people are cutting and burning them down, and digging them up.

Why? To make room for farms and ranches and roads. Or to mine or harvest their lumber and other natural resources. Some rain forests have been flooded by the building of dams.

rosy periwinkle

DID YOU KNOW?

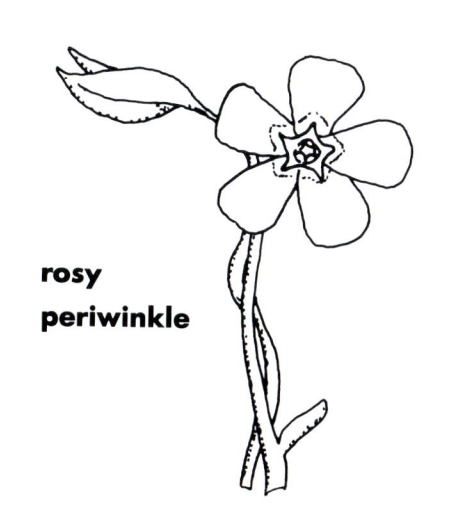

Many medicines come from plants of the tropical rain forests. A flower called the rosy periwinkle is used to fight blood cancer in children.

WHAT CAN YOU DO?

The United States has only a few tropical rain forests in Hawaii, Puerto Rico, and the Virgin Islands. But there are some things we can do to save all of the world's tropical rain forests.

▲ Join groups that are working to save tropical rain forests.
▲ Learn about tropical rain forests and the plants and animals that live in them. Read a book. Visit a zoo and a botanical garden. Tell others about what you learn.
▲ Don't buy rare tropical plants and animals taken from the wild.
▲ Say "no" to items made of tropical woods (mahogany, teak, and rosewood, for example).
▲ Don't eat cheap, "fast food" hamburgers and other meats that come from Central America. Many of these come from the meat of cattle raised on ranches that were carved out of a tropical forest. The cattle ruin the plants and soil after several years, so the ranchers carve out even more land from the rain forest. How can you tell where meat comes from? Ask! If the restaurant or butcher can't answer your question, don't eat or buy the meat.
▲ Ask your parents to support laws to protect tropical rain forests.

I CAN... ADOPT A PIECE OF EARTH

There are places near your home that could use some loving care too. Perhaps it's an overgrown lot full of trash near your house. Perhaps it's a small pond choked with weeds down the road. Or perhaps it's your own yard or the sidewalk in front of your apartment building.

WHAT CAN YOU DO?

Take pride in—and care of—your adopted piece of earth. Here's how:

▲ Keep your piece of earth clean. Pick up litter. Sweep the pavement.
▲ Pull out weeds. Rake up leaves.
▲ Mow the grass or sow some grass seed.
▲ Plant flowers, shrubs, and trees. If there is no soil, use large flower pots.
▲ Visit the spot often and keep coming back. Invite friends to join you.

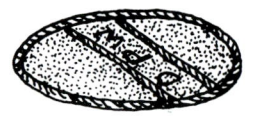

CHECK IT OUT

In nature there's no such thing as a weed. A weed is really just a wild plant out of place. Many animals, birds, and insects depend on weeds. However, if you want to get rid of an undesired plant, here are some tips to follow.

1. Get a trowel or a special weed tool.
2. Use the tool to loosen the soil underneath the weed.
3. Then pull out the weed. Be sure to get all the roots.
4. Add the weed to your compost pile if you have one.

WHAT'S THE DIFFERENCE?

▲ Imagine a stack of newspapers 20 feet high. That's how many newspapers the average American throws away each year. You'd have to chop down a 10-year-old tree to make this much paper. Or would you? Suppose you used old newspapers instead. Then you wouldn't need the tree and you can cut down on air and water pollution.

▲ An adult tree absorbs about 13 pounds of carbon dioxide a year. By planting 100 million trees, we could reduce carbon dioxide emissions by 18 million tons.

▲ The average family in the United States buys about 700 bags of groceries a year. It takes one 15-year-old tree to make 700 brown paper bags. If everybody used canvas bags instead of paper ones, we could save millions of trees a year.

▲ For every ton of paper that is made from recycled pulp, 17 trees are saved. Also that means less paper to take to the dump.

CHAPTER 6

FOR ANIMALS

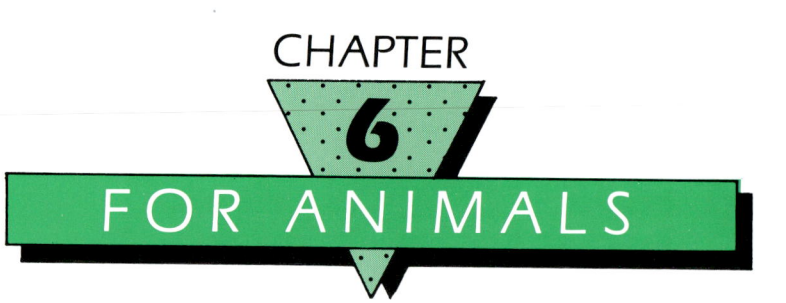

> **HOW CHILDREN CAN HELP THE WORLD**
>
> Room 3 is going to try and save part of the rain forest. Did you know that when one logging company cuts down a tree more than 1,000 animals are without a home?
>
> We are going to sell ice cold lemonade to raise money. We are going to try and raise up to 75 dollars. We are planning to send money to the wildlife company to save the rain forest.
>
> ROY CLOUD SCHOOL

Roy Cloud School is in Redwood City, California. The Room 3 students entered a contest about saving the world. They answered this question: "What can children do to help wild animals and the environment?" Do you like their idea?

DID YOU KNOW?

Many Native American groups had a special respect for animals. Some thought of them as brothers and sisters. Some honored them. Some Native Americans never killed animals unnecessarily. And some apologized to animals if they had to kill them for food or clothing.

We share this earth with many kinds of animals. Some are so tiny, they can live on a bug's back. Some are so big, they could sink a ship. Some are so strange, it would make you laugh. Some are so beautiful, they take your breath away.

No one knows for sure just how many kinds of animals there are on earth. But some scientists guess there are about 10 million—not 10 million individual animals but 10 million *types* of animals. There's no telling how many individual animals call earth their home. You couldn't count them if you spent your whole life trying.

Unfortunately, it seems that some people no longer want to share the world with all these animals. Each year people kill millions of wild animals.

Why are animals killed? Some are killed because people use them for food and clothing. Fur-bearing animals such as coyote, lynx, and beaver are killed for their coats, even though *we* don't need *their* skins to stay warm.

Some are killed because of carelessness and greed. Dolphins, for instance, often swim with schools of yellowfin tuna. Tuna ships follow dolphins to locate the tuna. When fishers throw nets out for tuna, they often trap and drown dolphins.

Pollution kills some animals. Many fish and other water animals and birds are dying for this reason. Some die because the water is dirty. Others try to eat the garbage floating in the water and die. Still others become entangled in invisible fishing nets that have been thrown away.

Most animals are dying because people are taking over the land the creatures once lived on. To make their livings, people build farms and cities and highways and factories. All these things take land—land that animals live on. When people take over a place, it's hard for animals to hang on. The plants they eat for food get destroyed. The spots they use for shelter are cut down. Many rain forest animals are dying out for this reason.

A WORD ABOUT ANIMAL RIGHTS

Some people are very sad about what's happening to the world's animals. They believe all animals are an important part of the web of life on earth. These people believe everyone should share the earth with animals and not harm them. They believe that no type of animal should disappear forever.

Other people don't seem to care much about animals. They think humans should always come first. If the animals get in the way of humans, they say, then the animals should go. Some people care so little about animals that they mistreat them.

Which kind of person are you? Do you care about animals? Do you think they have rights? If you care, turn to the next pages to find out ways you can help save the world's animals.

FIND IT OUT

Is there a special animal that you care about? Why not become an expert on it? Find out where it lives and what it eats. (Your library is full of books and magazines about animals.) Make a scrapbook about your favorite animal and fill it with pictures, poems, and stories. Then share your scrapbook with others. The more we learn about animals, the more we are able to help them.

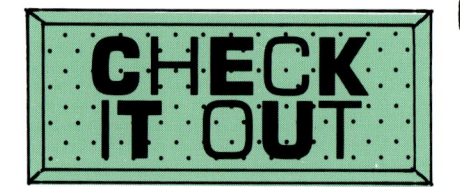

CHECK IT OUT

Animals are all around you—even if you live in the city. Take a walk around your neighborhood. Discover how many different types of animals you can find. Search for animals in trees, in the grass, near water, and even in the ground.

DID YOU KNOW?

Albert Schweitzer, a famous physician, wouldn't kill animals—not even bugs.

I CAN...
GIVE LOVING CARE TO PETS

Who doesn't love a puppy or a kitten? They're so cute and cuddly. They look like tiny stuffed toys. But pets are not like toys: They need lots of care—all of their lives. People shouldn't adopt a pet unless they have time to care for it . . . and love it.

WHAT CAN YOU DO?

▲ Feed pets regularly—once or twice a day, depending on their age and size. Ask your vet's advice. And keep your pets' dishes clean.

▲ Give your pets plenty of water. Keep the water bowl filled at all times. Change the water often to keep it fresh. And be sure it doesn't freeze in the winter, or dry up in the summer.

▲ Keep your pet clean, but get an adult's help. If necessary give your pet a soapy bath from time to time. Then rinse it thoroughly and dry it off well. Be sure the soap is earth-friendly. It should not be full of chemicals that are bad for you, your pet, or the earth.

▲ Keep your pet's coat nice. Brush and comb it often. Check the toenails and have an adult help you trim them.

▲ Keep fleas and ticks off your pet. Comb it often with a flea comb. (See "Try It Out.") Or bathe it with a flea soap or shampoo. Be sure to follow directions **exactly**. Try not to use flea collars and flea sprays. Many of these have poisons that may harm you and your pet.

▲ See that your pet gets plenty of exercise. If you don't have a yard for your dog to run in, take it for walks. But keep it on a leash.

▲ If you keep a pet indoors, make sure it has a place to go to the bathroom. Provide a litter box for your cat—and keep it clean. Let your dog out several times a day. If you will be gone for any length of time, leave newspapers in a corner area.

▲ Teach your pet to be polite and well behaved. Don't let it jump up on people or bite or scratch them. Don't let it damage furniture or dig up the lawn. Don't let its barking get out of control. But don't strike your pet when it is wrong. Instead, teach it with firm words. Say "no" or "down" when your pet is wrong. And praise your pet when it behaves.

▲ Take your pet to the animal doctor once a year for a checkup and shots. And ask your veterinarian about getting your pet "fixed." This means having an operation so it can't have babies.

▲ If you can't take care of your pet, find a caring, responsible family to give it to. If you can't do this, take it to an animal shelter or animal league. **Never** just stop feeding a pet or let it loose.

DID YOU KNOW?

In the United States, people own 50 million dogs and 58 million cats.

TRY IT OUT

Does your dog or cat have fleas? Forget the flea collar. Forget the flea spray. Bathe your pet in nonpoisonous, soapy water instead. Then comb it often with a flea comb. Here's how.

1. Comb your pet all over, starting at the head and neck.
2. When you see a flea on the comb, flick it into a bowl of soapy water.
3. Do this every day.

Also keep your pet's sleeping area clean. And vacuum the house often to get rid of flea eggs. Don't forget to toss out the vacuum bag afterward.

I CAN...
CARE ABOUT THE ANIMALS THAT AREN'T PETS

Most of us love animals. In fact, we love animals so much, we spend millions of dollars on them every year. But the animals most people love are pets. There are many other animals around us that deserve to receive better care.

For instance, millions of cows, calves, pigs, chickens, and turkeys are raised on farms for food. If they are lucky, they live on family farms. Then they are usually well cared for. But if they are unlucky, they live on "factory" farms. These are giant farms where lots of animals are raised together. Animals in these places don't get very good care at all.

Other nonpets, such as rats and rabbits and monkeys, are kept in cages in laboratories. There they are used for scientific research—to test products and drugs and medical methods. They lead miserable lives.

Some animals that aren't pets live in zoos and aquariums or travel with circuses. Others work for people—pulling carts or carrying passengers. Some of these animals are not treated very well, either.

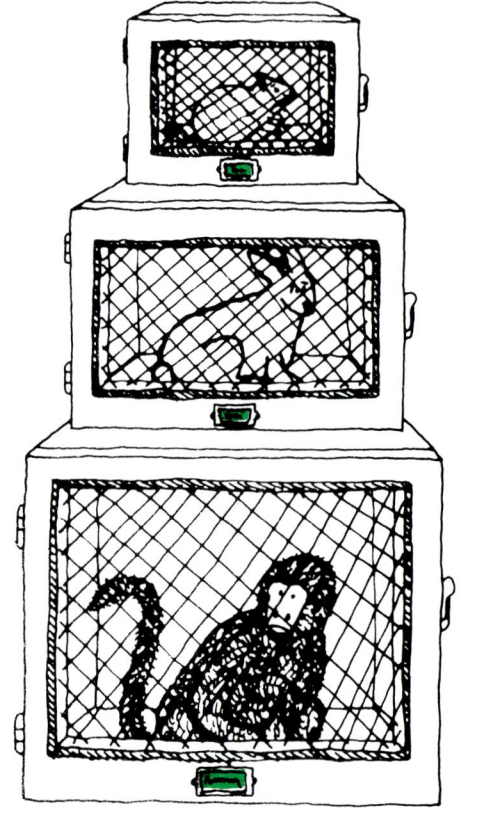

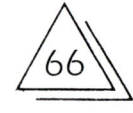

66

WHAT CAN YOU DO?

▲ If you see someone mistreating an animal, tell an adult immediately.

▲ Join a group that works to protect animals.

▲ Don't buy cosmetics and household products from companies that test products on animals. How can you tell? Some labels will state: Not Tested on Animals.

▲ Be kind to zoo animals. Don't feed them unless the zoo keeper says it's okay. And don't bother them by poking, whistling, or throwing things at them.

▲ If you live on a farm, take good care of your animals. Treat them the way you'd like to be treated if you were a farm animal.

A WORD ABOUT ZOOS AND AQUARIUMS

Some zoos and aquariums keep creatures in small, dirty cages and tanks. What we can hope is that enough visitors will complain and force these places to close. But many zoos and aquariums are working to help animals. A few are trying to raise rare animals that are in danger. They help them grow in numbers by giving them a safe place to have babies. Then they help them live in the wild.

How can you tell a good zoo from a poor zoo? First, a good zoo keeps animals in natural surroundings that look like the animal's original home. The cages and pens are kept clean. The animals are well fed. Often good zoos have educational programs that teach kids—and adults—about animals.

GALAPAGOS SEA LION
(Otaria byronia)

CHECK IT OUT

Next time you go to the store, check out the cosmetic section. Read the labels on shampoos, deodorants, lotions, and hair sprays. See which ones were not tested on animals. If your favorite products aren't cruelty-free, write the company or call its toll-free 800 number. Tell them what you think about testing on animals. Ask them to consider humane, or kind, alternatives.

I CAN... BE A FRIEND TO WILD ANIMALS

If you were a wild animal, which beast should you fear most—a tiger, a wolf, or a human being? The answer may surprise you. People kill far more wild animals than tigers and wolves.

Of course, hunters kill some of them. But most wild animals are killed by carelessness. People carelessly disturb animal nests, or destroy the places they live, or run over them on highways. Other animals are captured for sale as pets. Many of them don't make it alive to the pet store.

DID YOU KNOW?

Ivory comes from the tusks of elephants and walruses.

WHAT CAN YOU DO?

▲ Don't bother wild animals and don't disturb the places where they live.

▲ Don't trap, collect, or hunt wild animals. If you catch a wild animal to observe, be sure to put it back where it came from.

▲ Ask your parents to support laws to protect wild animals.

▲ Don't keep wild animals as pets. This means wild birds too. Many birds sold in pet stores were captured in forests. If you want a bird, make sure it was raised in captivity. How can you find out? Ask. Most hand-raised birds will be banded on their leg.

▲ If you find a sick or orphaned animal (one that has lost its mother), call a wildlife officer or a nature center. Don't touch or move it, or try to care for it yourself.

▲ Don't throw trash in places where animals live.

▲ Cut through plastic six-pack rings before you throw them away. Animals and birds can get caught in the rings and can become hurt or die.

▲ Don't let balloons loose. They often travel high up into the atmosphere and then come down in oceans where animals such as whales, dolphins, and turtles may mistake them for food, eat them, and become ill or die.

▲ Do not choose products made of ivory, feathers, tortoise shells, hides, and other wild animal parts. If you like the look and feel of wild fur and other animal belongings, buy fake.

▲ Visit zoos to learn about wild creatures.

▲ If you fish, follow all fishing laws. And return safely to the water any fish you don't really want to eat.

▲ Buy "dolphin-safe" tuna. A message will appear on the can like this:

DOLPHIN SAFE

▲ Keep dogs and cats in tow. Some dogs chase deer when allowed to roam. Many cats kill birds and other small animals. If your dog is a deer chaser, keep it on a leash or in the yard. If your cat is a hunter, put a bell on its collar.

DID YOU KNOW?

Each year about 100,000 dolphins are killed by tuna fishers. The dolphins get trapped in the tuna nets. The tuna in "dolphin-safe" cans are caught in a way that doesn't kill dolphins.

TEST IT OUT

Does a balloon look like a sea animal underwater? To find out, do this.

1. Get a fishbowl or fish tank, salt, water, and a balloon.
2. Fill the bowl with water. Add a little salt.
3. Toss in a balloon.
4. After several days, observe the balloon. Has its color changed? If the balloon were floating freely in the ocean, might it look like a fish?

I CAN...
FEED THE BIRDS

Feeding birds is a big hobby in the United States. Millions of people put out seeds and other treats for the birds. Some also put out birdhouses and birdbaths. Is this a good thing to do? You bet! If you've ever seen birds at a backyard feeder, you know they love these handouts. But first, there are a few things you should know about feeding birds.

70

DID YOU KNOW?

Most of the birds that visit backyard feeders are migratory birds. This means they spend summers in one place and winters in another. Many birds fly thousands of miles each year to get to their winter and summer homes.

WHAT CAN YOU DO?

▲ Follow a feeding schedule. Start feeding in the early fall and don't stop until early May. It's not fair to birds to get them used to being fed and then to stop—especially during the winter.

▲ Put out fresh bird food every day. Throw away food the birds don't eat before filling the feeder again. Food that lies around gets moldy and stale and can make birds sick.

▲ Put feeders up high—away from cats and other predators.

TRY IT OUT

You can make a bird feeder yourself. Here are two ideas.

▲ Stuff suet (animal fat) into a mesh bag. Tie a string around the top of the bag. Hang the feeder from a tree.

▲ Nail or glue pieces of wood around the edges of a board so that it makes a shallow box. Nail the board to a tree stump. Make sure there are bushes nearby in case the birds need to hide. Fill the feeder with wild bird seeds. (Most birds like sunflower seeds best.)

DID YOU KNOW?

Many birds love berries, fruits, and nuts. Yards that have berry bushes and fruit and nut trees attract more birds.

DID YOU KNOW?

Nearly 5,000 of the world's animal species are ENDANGERED, or in danger of dying out. About 600 of these animals are native to the United States.

WHAT CAN YOU DO?

▲ Be a friend to an endangered species. Practice all the rules you learned about saving wild animals. (See pg. 69.)

▲ Join a group that supports endangered animals.

▲ Join a group that has an adopt-an-animal program. The money you give will be used to help the animal.

▲ Send a donation to groups that buy land for animals.

I CAN... ADOPT AN ENDANGERED SPECIES

ANIMAL ALERT! ANIMAL ALERT! These animals are in danger. They are dying out. Something must be done. Something must be done *soon*. They need your help.

These are only a few of the thousands of animals in danger. Somewhere right now, as you read this book, another species (kind) is dying out. When an animal species dies out, it is gone forever. It becomes extinct—like the dinosaurs. A popular T-shirt slogan says it all: "Extinct is forever."

grizzly bear

northern spotted owl

DID YOU KNOW?

There are laws to protect animals in danger. There are also special places set aside for these animals to live. These places are called wildlife refuges. About 35 refuges have been set aside to protect endangered animals.

FIND IT OUT

Here is a list of some groups working to save wildlife. Write these groups to find out how you can adopt and help animals.

Adopt-an-Acre Program
The Nature Conservancy
1815 North Lynn Street
Arlington, VA 22209

Adopt an Animal
San Francisco Zoological Society
1 Zoo Road
San Francisco, CA 94132-1098

The Alaska Wildlife Alliance
P.O. Box 202022
Anchorage, AL 99520

The Children's Rain Forest
P.O. Box 936
Lewiston, ME 04240

Defenders of Wildlife
1244 19th Street NW
Washington, DC 20036

Earth Island Institute
300 Broadway
Suite 28
San Francisco, CA 94133

The Fund for Animals
200 West 57 Street
New York, NY 10019

Greenpeace
1436 U Street NW
Suite 201-A
Washington, DC 20009

Whale Adoption Project
634 North Falmouth Highway
P.O. Box 388
North Falmouth, MA 02556

Wildlife Conservation International
New York Zoological Society
Bronx, NY 10460-9973

World Wildlife Fund
1250 24th Street NW
Washington, DC 20037

DID YOU KNOW?

These are some of the animals in danger of dying out:

African and Asian elephants
American crocodile
Anegada ground iguana
Bengal tiger
Black-footed ferret
Brown pelican
California condor
Cheetah
Chimpanzee
Florida Key deer
Florida panther
Gray wolf
Grizzly bear
Humpback whale
Jaguar
Leopard
Louisiana black bear
Mountain gorilla
Mountain zebra
Northern spotted owl
Ocelot
Orangutan
Panda
Prairie dog
Rhinoceros
Sea turtle
Southern bald eagle
Southern sea otter

humpback whale

sea turtles

WHAT'S THE DIFFERENCE?

▲ Millions of cats and dogs are abandoned every year. Most end up on the streets or in shelters. Most die of hunger or disease, or are put to sleep because they are unwanted. Every day, more unwanted animals are born. If you spay or neuter your animals (so they can't have babies) and give them loving care, you will help end this misery.

▲ Each animal on earth has a place in nature. Think of the beaver. Perhaps its place is to make homes for other creatures. Think of the hawk and the wolf. Perhaps their place is to prey upon other animals to keep the number of those animals under control. Think of the bee. Perhaps its place is to spread pollen from plant to plant.

When one species of animals dies out, its place in nature is lost. This upsets nature's balance. For instance, suppose all the beavers vanished. There wouldn't be any more beaver ponds. Then ducks and frogs and other water creatures would have fewer places to live.

When an animal becomes extinct, it is a tragedy for nature. It is also a warning for people that something is wrong with the earth.

▲ Wild birds don't really need you to feed them. They can get their food from nature. But they enjoy eating from backyard feeders. When you feed birds, you are showing that you care—and this is good news for the birds. It's good news for you, too, because birds are lots of fun to listen to and watch.

▲ Do you know the story of Noah and the Ark? According to the Bible, Noah learned from God that a big flood was coming. Noah wanted to save the animals, so he built a large boat called an ark. Of course, Noah couldn't take all of the animals, but he led a pair (a male and female) of each species on to the ark. After the flood was over, Noah let the animals go. In time the animals had babies and their babies had babies. Soon the animals were spread out over the land again. Each time people save a pair of animals, they are saving a little bit of the future.

CHAPTER 7
FOR KID POWER

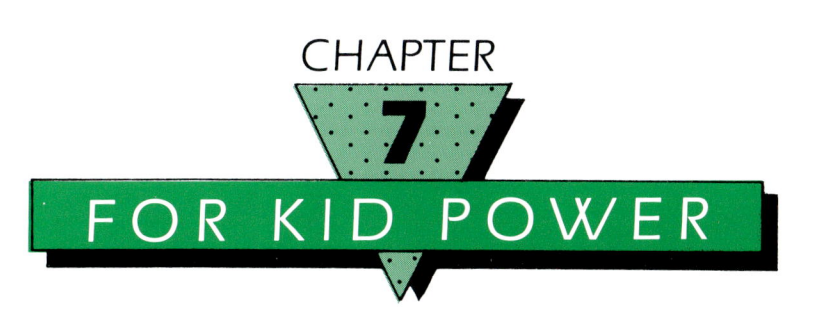

Are the problems described in this book really bothering you? Are you worried that not enough is being done? Do you sometimes feel helpless about it all? Think positive. And take action. Kids DO have power. Kids CAN make a difference. In this chapter are lots of ideas about ways you can use *your* power to save the earth.

DID YOU KNOW?

One of the first environmental groups in the United States was the Sierra Club. It was founded by John Muir, a famous naturalist, in 1892. In its long history, it has worked to save wild areas, wild plants, wild animals, and resources that are in danger.

A WORD ABOUT ACTIONS THAT COUNT

I CAN SAVE THE EARTH

In the year 1970 people who cared about the earth held the first Earth Day. It was a party for the earth. During the celebration, many people and companies promised to help the earth.

Did Earth Day make a difference? Did people keep their promises? You decide. Here are some of the changes that have happened since 1970.

▲ We have more than twice as many national parklands and wilderness areas.

▲ Pollution laws got tougher.

▲ Gasoline got cleaner. Lead, a dangerous chemical, was removed from gasoline.

▲ Coal users had to stop using coal with lots of polluting sulfur in it.

▲ Cars got more energy-efficient. They go farther on a gallon of gas.

▲ The air got cleaner in many cities. Air pollution is still a big problem. But air doesn't have as much dirty soot as it once did.

▲ Electrical appliances got more energy-efficient. They use less electricity than they used to.

▲ Most neighborhoods used to take their garbage to dumps. At dumps, garbage lies on top of the ground. Dumps are smelly and dirty. Now most trash is taken to landfills. In landfills, garbage is covered with dirt each day.

▲ People recycle more.

▲ More people care about the earth. There are more environmental groups.

▲ More companies make earth-friendly products. Fewer companies use animals for tests.

▲ Some of the most dangerous pesticides have been outlawed.

▲ Fewer people wear fur coats. In the 1970s, fur coats were "in." Now they are "out."

How did all these changes come about? People who care about the earth made them happen. People held rallies. People wrote letters. People voted for government leaders who promised to pass laws to help the earth. People refused to buy things from companies that hurt the earth. In the next 20 years, even more can happen—if you and others carry on the I-can-save-the-earth message.

FIND IT OUT

How has your town changed since Earth Day? Are things better? Worse? The same? Or just different? Interview lots of people to find out. Start with your family, relatives, and neighbors. And keep a record. Here's how.

1. Get a tape recorder and a pencil and pad.
2. Write down some questions you want to ask.
3. Pick a time and place to do each interview. The place should be quiet. You should allow at least a half hour for talking.
4. Turn on the tape recorder. Then ask your first question. Give the person plenty of time to answer. If you don't understand the answer, get the person to explain it better.
5. Keep asking questions until you find out everything you want to know.
6. Thank the person for the interview.

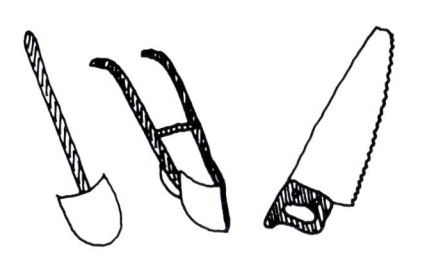

DID YOU KNOW?

Machines help people do a lot of work fast. But machines can also damage the earth a lot faster than people can. A steam shovel can dig up a lot more land than a hand shovel. A tractor can plow a lot more land than a shovel or hand plow. A chainsaw can saw down a lot more trees than a handsaw. When people use machines, they need to make sure they don't damage the earth.

I CAN...
JOIN OR START A GROUP

You're not the only person in the country who wants to save the earth. There are millions of people who feel the same way as you do. Many of these people have joined groups to help save the earth. Some groups work to save the air. Some work to save water. Some work to save wild places or animals. There is probably a group just right for you.

77

WHAT CAN YOU DO?

▲ Find out the names and addresses of groups in your town or state. Look in a phone book. Or ask a teacher or librarian to help you.

▲ Find out the names and addresses of national groups. Some names are on pg. 79. For more names, send fifty cents to:

Sierra Club
730 Polk Street
San Francisco, CA 94109

▲ Write a letter to the groups that interest you most. Ask how to become a member. Ask what the group does and how much it costs to join. Be sure to tell them your age. Some groups have special rates for kids.

▲ Decide what groups you like best. Then join.

▲ If you can't find a group that's working for what you're interested in, start your own group. Many kids like Melissa Poe have. Her group, Kids For a Clean Environment (Kids F.A.C.E.), has more than 10,000 members.

FIND IT OUT

It costs at least $15 to join many of these groups. If you can't afford the membership fee, you might share it with a friend.

Kids F.A.C.E.
P.O. Box 158254
Nashville, TN 37215

Friends of the Earth
218 D Street SE
Washington, DC 20003

Mothers and Others
40 West 20th Street
New York, NY 10011

National Audubon Society
950 Third Avenue
New York, NY 10027

National Wildlife Federation
1412 16th Street NW
Washington, DC 20036-2266

Rainforest Action Network
301 Broadway
San Francisco, CA 94133

Sierra Club
730 Polk Street
San Francisco, CA 94109

Student Conservation Association, Inc.
P.O. Box 550
Charlestown, NH 03630

The Wilderness Society
1400 I Street NW
Washington, DC 20005

This list should not be considered as an endorsement of the goals or methods of any groups.

I CAN... FIND OUT ABOUT THINGS AND TELL OTHERS

"Gee, I didn't know that." That's an excuse you often hear. But these days "I didn't know" is not a very good excuse.

We live in a world of information. It's all around us. We get information from TV, radio, newspapers, magazines, books, schools, libraries, and from listening to other people. People who don't know things just aren't listening or reading. If you care about the earth, you need to find out about many things. But always question everything you find out. Don't take anybody's word without thinking about it and checking it out for yourself.

WHAT CAN YOU DO?

▲ Read magazines. Lots of kids' magazines write about nature and the environment. Some good magazines to check out are: *Ranger Rick, 3-2-1 Contact, National Geographic World, Zillions, Skipping Stones,* and *P-3, The Earth-based Magazine for Kids.* Many environmental groups also put out magazines for kids.

▲ Read the newspapers. Some of the articles may be hard to understand, but you can get lots of information by reading headlines and skimming the stories. Ask your parents to explain a news article. Discuss it with them.

▲ Listen to the news on radio and TV.

▲ Watch special environmental programs on network or cable TV. Some of these programs are made especially for kids.

▲ Read books. Your librarian can help you find the books you need.

▲ Borrow videos from the local video store, or better still, borrow them from your library.

▲ Go to town meetings. Find out what's going on in your community.

▲ Visit museums, zoos, nature centers, parks, and botanical gardens.

▲ Study the environment in your science class at school.

▲ Talk to people. Ask questions.

▲ Be a good observer. Pay attention to what's going on around you. You'll be surprised about how much you learn.

I CAN... LET OTHERS KNOW WHAT I THINK

Is something bothering you? Are things happening that you don't like or that worry you? What will you do about it? Grumbling won't help if you don't let the right people know what you think. While kids don't have a vote, they **do** have a voice. And what they say **can** make a difference.

WHAT CAN YOU DO?

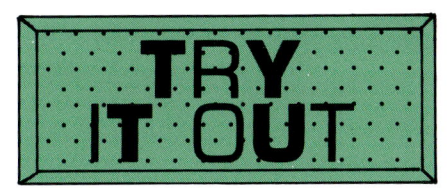

▲ Write a letter to the editor of your local newspaper. Give your name (if you want to) and your age. If you keep writing, maybe the editor will print your letter in the "Letters to the Editor" column.

▲ Write to a government official. You can write your United States senator or congressperson or even the president. Just as important, you can write to the leaders of your town. They're usually very interested in what the residents have to say.

▲ Write to a company that's doing something to the earth that you don't like. Companies want to make customers happy. If they find out that people don't like what they're doing, chances are they'll stop.

TRY IT OUT

It's easy to write a good letter. Here is the proper way to write an official:

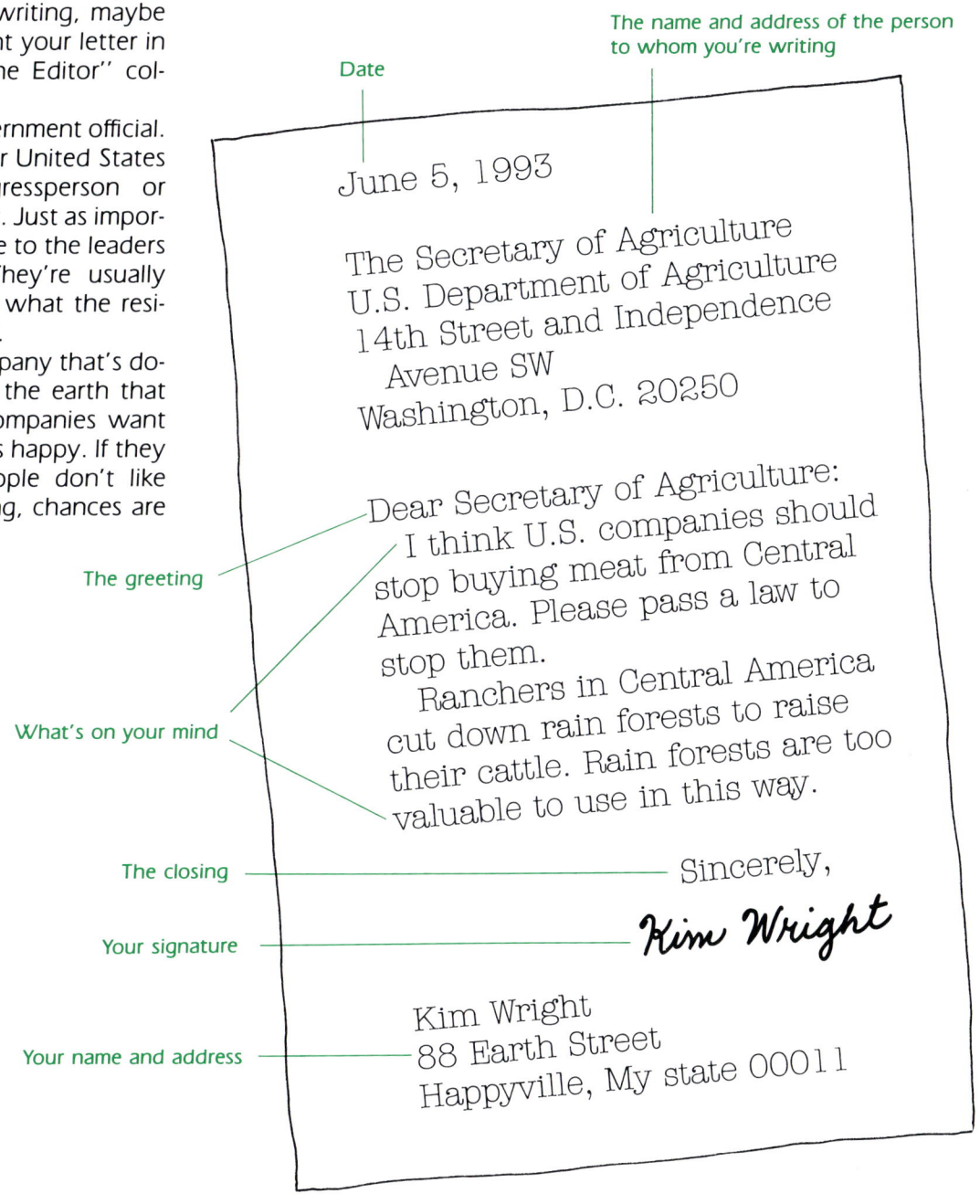

Date

The name and address of the person to whom you're writing

June 5, 1993

The Secretary of Agriculture
U.S. Department of Agriculture
14th Street and Independence Avenue SW
Washington, D.C. 20250

The greeting

Dear Secretary of Agriculture:

What's on your mind

I think U.S. companies should stop buying meat from Central America. Please pass a law to stop them.

Ranchers in Central America cut down rain forests to raise their cattle. Rain forests are too valuable to use in this way.

The closing — Sincerely,

Your signature — Kim Wright

Your name and address

Kim Wright
88 Earth Street
Happyville, My state 00011

I CAN... TAKE ACTION

Suppose you found out that your town leaders were planning to pave over a beautiful meadow full of wild flowers and songbirds. Their reason? To build a parking lot. What would you do?

You could shake your head and do nothing. You could complain to your friends. Or you could take a stand. You could protest directly to the town leaders and get others to join you. Sometimes, to make things right, we have to take action. We have to let government leaders or business leaders know how we feel. And sometimes we have to encourage others to join us in our action. There are lots of ways to get action from government leaders.

WHAT CAN YOU DO?

▲ Start a letter-writing campaign. Get a bunch of people to write letters about the problem.

▲ Write a petition about the problem. Get lots of people to sign it. Send the petition to a government leader.

▲ Hold a rally about the problem. Carry posters or pass out flyers that tell others what you think. Get lots of people to come. But get an adult to help you organize the rally.

▲ Stop buying products that are harming the earth. Explain to others why you're doing this. Maybe they'll stop buying too. Write the manufacturer to explain your position.

CHECK IT OUT

How can you let others know about an action you're planning? You can pass out leaflets. You can telephone people. Or you can put up signs or posters. A good sign catches everybody's eye. It attracts attention. It also gives all the important information. It tells when, where, and why. Make sure you place your sign where it will not offend others or break the laws of your community. Perhaps your town has a community bulletin board.

I CAN...
SET AN EXAMPLE

Here's an old saying; "Actions speak louder than words." It means that what we do is often more important than what we say. For instance, if you tell someone not to cheat on a test, and you yourself cheat, he or she probably won't pay much attention to you.

"Practice what you preach" is another old saying that makes a lot of sense. What it means is that people should do what they tell others to do. Both sayings add up to the same thing: If we want others to follow our advice, we must set a good example.

WHAT CAN YOU DO?

If you want people around you to be good to the earth, first you must be good to it yourself. But don't expect instant results. And don't expect praise or rewards. Being good to the earth is a way of life . . . and is it's own reward.

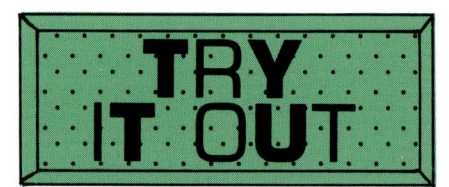

TRY IT OUT

Can you set an example for others? Think of a bad habit that you have—one that hurts the earth. Perhaps it's wasting water, littering, or leaving on the lights in an empty room. Decide to change your bad habit and keep your promise. Chances are, if you keep it up, others around you will get the message. Before you know it, they may follow in your footsteps.

WHALES ARE IMPORTANT

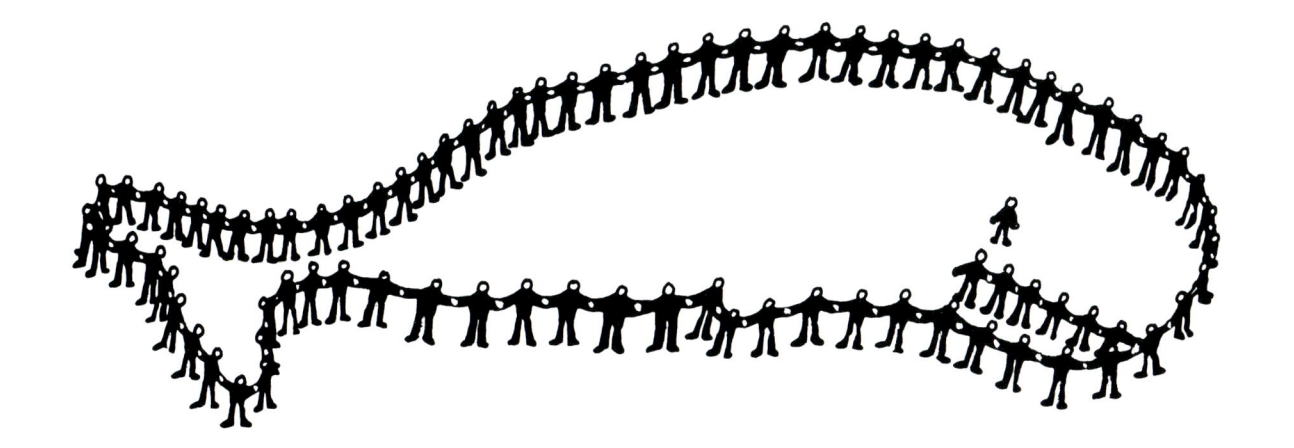

WHAT'S THE DIFFERENCE?

Here are some ways kids have worked together to make a difference.

▲ Laura Nelson is an Aurora, Colorado, girl who knows all about taking action. She learned that dolphins often get killed when fishers fish for tuna. Laura couldn't stand the idea of dolphins being killed. So she decided to do something about it.

First Laura wrote a petition. It asked the school cafeteria to stop serving tuna. She got lots of kids to sign it. Then she took the petition to the school board. Eventually, the school board listened. In time, all the schools in her town stopped serving tuna.

Laura was only one of many kids across the country who worked to save dolphins. Eventually, so many kids and grown-ups stopped buying tuna that the tuna companies got the message. Today many tuna companies sell only "dolphin-safe" tuna. This means that the tuna was caught without injuring and killing dolphins.

▲ Kids at Oak Creek Elementary School in Houston, Texas, wanted to help Ridley turtles. These tiny sea turtles are in danger of dying out. Why? They lay their eggs on beaches in Mexico. People steal the eggs for souvenirs.

The Oak Creek kids started a group. The group is called HEART (Help Endangered Animals—Ridley Turtles). HEART raises money. The money is given to scientists who raise Ridley turtles in a safe place.

▲ Kids in Lancaster, New Hampshire, formed a group called the BLTs (Balloon Launch Terminators). They get people to stop letting balloons loose in the air. Why? To protect ocean animals.

▲ A group of kids in Massachusetts care a lot about whales. They stood side by side to form the shape of a whale. They sent a photo to the local newspaper. Readers got the message: "Whales are important."

▲ In Bloomfield, California, kids care about rain forests. They formed a rain forest committee. The committee recycles aluminum cans. It sells the cans to a recycling company. Then it contributes the money to save rain forest land.

Kids in many other towns also donate money to save rain forests. Some collect money from friends, family, and teachers. Some earn the money by doing chores, or by making things and selling them. It takes about $130 to buy an acre of rain forest.

▲ Kids in South Hadley, Massachusetts, recycle envelopes. But they found out that envelopes with plastic windows can't be recycled. So they took action. They wrote to companies that use the envelopes. The letter said, "Please do not use envelopes with plastic windows."

THE ECO RAP

I'M THE RAPPIN' ECO MAN
AND I'M HERE TO SAY:
WE NEED TO SAVE THE EARTH—
AND I MEAN TODAY!

I'VE BEEN TO THE FUTURE,
I'VE BEEN TO THE PAST;
I'VE COME TO THE CONCLUSION
THERE'S TOO MUCH TRASH

THAT IS ALL WE HAVE TO SAY,
BUT WE'LL COME BACK ANOTHER DAY!

John Thomas Fitzgerald
St. Louis, MO

FURTHER READING

Brown, Richard A. *A Kid's Guide to National Parks.* San Diego, CA: Harcourt, Brace Jovanovich, 1989.

Crump, Donald J., ed. *Adventures in Your National Parks.* Washington, D.C.: National Geographic Society, 1989.

Curtis, Patricia. *All Wild Creatures Welcome: The Story of a Wildlife Rehabilitation Center.* New York: Dutton, 1985.

Gardner, Robert. *The Whale Watchers' Guide.* New York: Julian Messner, 1984.

George, Jean Craighead. *One Day in the Tropical Rain Forest.* New York: Crowell, 1990.

Gibbons, Gail. *Recycle! A Handbook for Kids.* New York: Little, Brown, 1992.

Hamilton, Jean. *Tropical Rainforests.* San Luis Obispo, CA: Blake Publishing, 1990.

Huff, Barbara A. *Greening the City Streets: The Story of Community Gardens.* New York: Clarion Books, 1990.

Markmann, Erika. *Grow It! An Indoor-Outdoor Gardening Guide for Kids.* New York: Random House, 1991.

Miller, Christina G. and Berry, Louise A. *A Coastal Rescue: Preserving Our Seashores.* New York: Macmillan, 1989.

Miller, Christina G. and Berry, Louise A. *A Jungle Rescue: Saving the New World Tropical Rainforests.* New York: Macmillan, 1991.

Mitchell, A. *The Young Naturalist.* Tulsa, OK: Educational Development Corporation, 1984.

Patent, Dorothy H. *The Challenge of Extinction.* Hillside, NJ: Enslow Publishers, 1991.

Pearce, Q.L. *Piranhas and Other Wonders of the Jungle.* New York: Julian Messner, 1990.

Pfeffer, Wendy. *Popcorn Park Zoo: A Haven with a Heart.* New York: Julian Messner, 1992.

Pringle, Laurence. *Living Treasure: Saving Earth's Threatened Biodiversity.* New York: Morrow, 1991.

Robinson, W. Wright. *Incredible Facts About the Ocean. Volume 3: How We Use It, How We Abuse It.* New York: Macmillan, 1990.

Savan, Beth. *Earthwatch: Earthcycles and Ecosystems.* Menlo Park, CA: Addison-Wesley, 1992.

Schwarz, Linda. *Likeable Recyclables: Creative Ideas for Reusing Bags, Boxes, Cans, and Cartons.* Santa Barbara, CA: The Learning Works, 1990.

Steele, Philip. *Extinct Birds: And Those in Danger of Extinction.* New York: Franklin Watts, 1991.

Stwertka, Eve and Albert. *Cleaning Up: How Trash Becomes Treasure.* New York: Julian Messner, 1993.

Stwertka, Eve and Albert. *Drip Drop: Water's Journey.* New York: Julian Messner, 1991.

Tolan, Sally. *John Muir: Naturalist, Writer and Guardian of the North American Wilderness.* Milwaukee, WI: Gareth Stevens, Inc. 1989.

Whitfield, Philip. *Can the Whales Be Saved?* New York: Viking, 1989.

GLOSSARY

acid rain—rain that picks up harmful chemicals from polluted air

aerosol can—a can that sprays things in the air by means of squeezed up gas

algae—very simple plants that generally live in water

atmosphere—the invisible blanket of air that surrounds the earth

biodegradable—able to rot or turn back to soil

carbon dioxide—a colorless, odorless gas made of carbon and oxygen. Carbon dioxide is a natural part of air, but too much can cause climate problems. Carbon dioxide is a waste gas produced when living things breathe out, when things are burned, and when things rot.

combustion—burning

compost—leaves, other plant parts, and garbage left to rot; compost helps make soil more fertile

conservation—not wasting

conserve—save, keep, protect

detergents—cleaners made from human-made chemicals, not natural ones

earth-friendly—doesn't hurt the earth

ecology—the study of living things and their surroundings

endangered—in danger of dying out; when a type of animal or plant dies out, it's gone forever.

energy—the power to move or do something

environment—the land, water, and air surrounding us, and everything that's on the land and in the water and air

fuel—something that is burned for energy. Wood, coal, oil, and natural gas are fuels.

global warming—a warming of the earth's climates caused by air pollution. Waste gases trap heat from the sun. This warms up the air around the earth. Also called the greenhouse effect.

groundwater—all the water that's in soil and stored underground

incinerator—a furnace used for burning trash

insulation—a material that traps heat

kilowatt—one thousand watts

landfill—a huge pit for burying trash and garbage

litter—trash that's carelessly scattered about

national park—a park owned by the national government; thus, a park owned by the people of the country

oxygen—the colorless, odorless, tasteless gas in air that people and other living things need to breathe; trees and plants produce oxygen.

ozone layer—a band of gas 30 to 40 miles away from earth. This layer of gas protects earth from the dangerous rays of the sun.

pesticide—pest-killer, usually from human-made chemicals

pollute—to make dirty and unhealthful, to poison

recycle—to use again

solid waste—waste that's solid, like trash and garbage

tropical rain forest—a forest in the rainy, warm parts of earth often called the tropics

watt—a unit for measuring electricity; two watts is enough to run a clock.

wetland—land that is always or often covered by water. Swamps, marshes, and bogs are different kinds of wetlands.

wild plant—one that grows freely in nature

wilderness—a wild place—usually uncultivated and uninhabited— where plants and animals grow freely

INDEX

Acid rain, 12, 89
Aerosol can, 89
Air pollution, 8–10, 19, 21
Airwaves, 20
Algae, 89
Aluminum, 36, 42
Aluminum foil, 41, 42
Animals
    pets, 65–66
    rights, 63
    testing of products on, 68
    types of, 62
    water, 25, 31, 62–74
    wild, 46, 68–69
Appliances, 12, 13
Aquariums, 67
Atmosphere, 89

Bags, 41, 53, 61
Baths, 27
Beavers, 74
Bicycles, 10, 38
Biodegradable, 36, 44, 89
Birds, 70–71, 74

Cans, see Containers
Canvas bags, 53, 61
Carbon dioxide, 8, 10, 55, 89
Carpools, 10, 11
Cars, 10
Cats, 65–66, 69, 74
Cattle, 59
Central America, 59
Chemicals, 18, 32, 39
Choices, 6–7
Christmas trees, 51
Cigarettes, 19
Cleaners, 28–39
Climate zones, 49
Clothing, 44
Coal, 12
Combustion, 89
Compost, 40, 43, 89
Conservation, 89
<u>Consumer Reports</u>, 37
Containers, 40–42
Cups, 41

Detergents, 29, 89
Dirt bikes, 52
Dogs, 65–66, 69, 74
Dolphins, 62, 69, 70, 85
Drafts, 14, 15

Earth Day, 76, 77
Earth-friendly, 89
Ecology, 90
Electricity, 10–13
Electric meter, 13
Endangered species, 72–73, 90
Energy, 9, 11–14, 90
Environment, 6, 90
Exhaust fumes, 10
Extinct species, 74

Faucets, 27, 28, 32
Feeders, 71
Fleas, 65–66
Flowers, 46, 55
Foil, see Aluminum foil
Forests, 6, 46, 50, 53, 57–59, 85, 91
Fuel, 11, 90

Garbage, see Trash
Gasoline, 10, 21
Gift wrap, 54
Global warming, 90
Green, 4, 5
Groundwater, 23, 90
Groups and organizations, 77–79, 85

Hand-me-downs, 44
Hard water, 29
Heat, 14, 15
Hot water, 16, 17

Incinerator, 90
Information, 79, 83
Insulation, 13, 90
Internal combustion, 90

Jars, see Containers
Jungles, 46

"**K**id power," 7, 75–85
Kilowatts, 12, 90

Labels, 18
Land care, 33, 60
Landfill, 90
Leaflets, 83
Letter writing, 81, 82
Lights, 12, 13
Litter, 7, 31, 34, 90

Machines, 9, 77
Magazines, 37, 80
Mass transit, 10
Meats, 59
Metal, 37
Muir, John, 75

National parks, see Parks
Native Americans, 62
Natural resources, 33, 34
Nature, 4, 5
News, 80
Newspapers, 54, 61, 80
Newsprint, 55
Noah's Ark, 74
Noise, 20, 21

Oceans, 22, 31
Oil, 10, 11
Organizations, see Groups and organizations
Oxygen, 8, 55, 90
Ozone layer, 20, 91

Packaging, 37, 40–41
Paper, 39, 40, 53, 61
Parks, 4, 47–49, 58, 90
Pesticide, 91
Petitions, 82, 85
Pets, 65–66

93

Phosphates, 29
Plants, 55
    around water edges, 31
    compost, 43
    rare, 56
    wild, 48, 49, 91
Plastic foam (polystyrene), 41
Plastics, 37, 39–40, 41
Pollution, 6, 91
    air, 8–10
    and animals, 62
    catcher, 9
    checker, 9
    chemical, 31
    water, 22–23, 30–31

Rain, 23–24
Rain forests, 58–59, 85, 91
Recycling, 33, 39–45, 54, 85, 91
Refrigerators, 12
Resources, see Natural resources
Reuse, see Recycling
Rivers, 30, 31, 57
Rust, 37

Salt water, 22, 25
Schweitzer, Albert, 64
Seashores, 47–49
Showers, 27
Sierra Club, 75
Smoking, 19

Soaps, 28, 29
Soil, 49
Solid waste, 34, 91
Sound, 20, 21
Summer, 14
Sun, 17, 20

Tag sale, 45
Temperature, 13–14
Thermostat, 14
Throwaways, 38–41
Tobacco, 19
Toilets, 27–28
Tooth brushing, 32
Toys, 37, 38
Trash, 6, 33–38, 42, 43
Trees, 50–52, 54, 61
Tropical forests, 57–59, 91
Tuna, 62, 69, 70, 85

Warning labels, 18
Waste, see Trash
Water
    creatures, 25, 31
    fresh, 22
    guzzlers, 16
    hard, 29
    hot, 16, 17
    leaks, 16
    pollution, 22–23, 30–31
    salty, 22, 25
    supply, 22
    uses, 24
    wastage, 26–28, 31
Waterfowl, 31
Watts, 12, 91
Weeds, 61
Wetlands, 31–32, 46, 57, 91
Wild animals, 46, 68–69
Wild flowers, 55, 56
Wildlife refuges, 72
Wild places, 56–58
Wild plants, 46, 49, 91
Winter, 14

Zillions, 37
Zoos, 67

ABOUT THE AUTHOR AND ILLUSTRATOR

Anita Holmes, the author, has written numerous articles for children on science, nature, and the environment. Her books include *100-Year-Old Cactus*; *Cactus, the All-American Plant*; *Plant Fun: 10 Easy Plants to Grow Indoors*; and *Flowers for You*. Ms. Holmes is co-founder of the Endangered Species Committee of the New York chapter of the Sierra Club and is a charter member of the Friends of the Earth. In 1970, she received the Cachet Award for environmental achievement.

Ms. Holmes resides in Norfolk, Connecticut.

David Neuhaus, the illustrator, received a degree in illustration from the Parsons School of Design in New York City. He has received awards from the Society of Illustrators and the Illustrators Club in Washington, D.C. He has illustrated *Helga High Up*, *Sherman Is a Slowpoke*, *The Halloween Grab Bag*, and *The Drug-Alert Series*, and has written and illustrated *His Finest Hour*.

Mr. Neuhaus is a senior designer at a New York children's publishing house and lives with his wife Susan and daughter Sophie in Fanwood, New Jersey.

NOTES

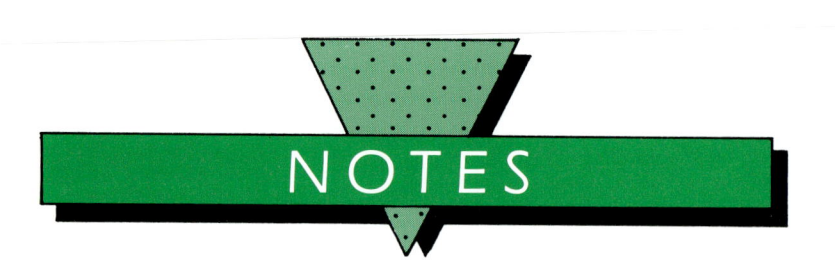